DOWNTON ABBEY

A NEW ERA

THE OFFICIAL FILM COMPANION

EMMA MARRIOTT

weldon**owen**

CONTENTS

FOREWORD

HAVING SUCCESSFULLY MIGRATED THE SERIES TO THE BIG SCREEN, what a pleasure it is to welcome you back to *Downton Abbey*. Woven into the film's storyline are two exciting new elements: The ancestral home of the Crawleys is turned into a film set and provides the backdrop for an early "talking picture." At the same time, members of the family and staff have decamped to the fashionable sunny climes of the French Riviera, this foreign expedition being a first for the series and something quite special.

The film features a host of new characters played by Dominic West, Laura Haddock, Hugh Dancy, Nathalie Baye and Jonathan Zaccaï, all of whom deliver superb performances. As always, however, the Crawley family and the staff who serve them are at the heart of *Downton Abbey*. Whatever challenges appear, they are the ones who work around the problem and save the day. When it looks as though the film production is about to fall apart, Lady Mary steps in to provide her voice for one of the characters, Molesley reworks the script and the staff are drafted to serve as movie extras. In France, Robert finds himself in a very alien environment and must wrestle with some earth-shattering news. And throughout the film we see the resolution of various romances, from the joyful wedding of Tom Branson and Lucy to the eventual promise of a happy ending for Barrow, for whom audiences have been rooting for the past decade or more.

The overriding story, perhaps, is that of the Dowager Countess. The film opens with Violet alone at the Abbey, now too frail to attend Tom and Lucy's wedding and ends with a close-up of her portrait in the hall watching over the younger members of the family, just as Mary predicted she one day would at the end of the previous film. Dame Maggie Smith is, of course, remarkable and her final scenes are testament both to her standing as one of our greatest actresses and to the creative chemistry that exists between her and Julian Fellowes. While it may seem as if she were a permanent presence on *Downton Abbey*, the truth is that when we were making the television series we never knew for certain whether she would be returning each year. We were always in the somewhat bizarre situation of working on scripts until quite late in the day, only to breathe a huge sigh of relief when she finally said yes and we knew she was on board. The wait was always well worth it. Nonetheless, as Violet herself is all too aware, the time has come for her to pass on the mantle. *Downton Abbey* is set to embark on a new era and I am delighted to welcome you to it.

Gareth Neame
Producer, *Downton Abbey*
London, 2021

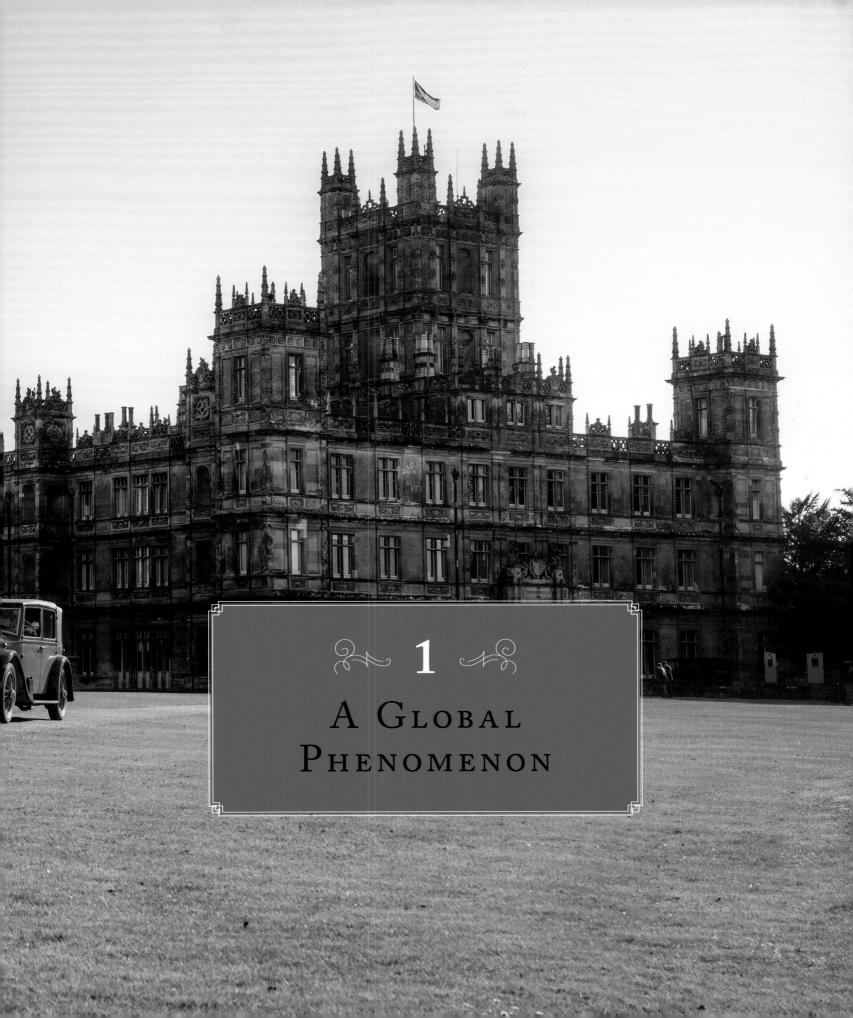

1

A GLOBAL PHENOMENON

> "You travel thousands and thousands of miles,
> and you get off a plane and someone says,
> 'Is Mr. Carson going to marry Mrs. Hughes?'"

—JULIAN FELLOWES

Followers of *Downton Abbey* of course know full well that Mr. Carson does, eventually, marry Mrs. Hughes, and those fans, as Julian Fellowes testifies, may be found almost anywhere in the world. Since 2010, the six seasons of *Downton Abbey* have aired in over 250 territories around the globe, with fans from Seattle to Shanghai, and from Brisbane to Bonn, tuning in by the millions to catch up on the continuing fortunes of the Crawley household. By 2016, after the final season aired in the United Kingdom, *Downton Abbey* had earned itself three Golden Globes, fifteen Emmys, four Screen Actors Guild awards, and a BAFTA Television Special Award. It was, quite simply, one of the most successful television dramas ever made.

After a three-year hiatus and fevered speculation, *Downton Abbey* returned as a movie in 2019. Enthusiasm for the film release had mounted, as was evident during test screenings when audiences began cheering at the first sight of the familiar turrets of Highclere Castle accompanied by the pulsating rhythm of the *Downton* music. In the United States and the United Kingdom, the movie topped the box office in its opening weekend, knocking Brad Pitt and Sylvester Stallone features off the top spot. The *Downton Abbey* movie earned more than $193 million at the worldwide box office, making it the highest grossing film of all time for its distributor Focus Features.

On the back of such success, it's no surprise that plans were put in place for a second movie, one that featured all the ingredients that have made *Downton* an enduring success but scaled up in a new setting and scenario. *Downton Abbey*'s creators, principally producer Gareth Neame and writer Julian Fellowes, had a few ideas up their sleeves as to how they might achieve that, part of which involved taking *Downton Abbey* to an exciting new location.

"Some of the Christmas Day episodes we did for the series, where we went to the Highlands of Scotland, Northumberland, or London for the season, had a really special feel about them," explains Neame. "I had always wanted to take *Downton Abbey* to the French Riviera—in the 1920s our characters would have been traveling there, and in fact we learn that Violet went there as a young woman in the nineteenth century, so it seemed entirely credible. So when Julian and I began talking about what the story of a second film might be, I pushed for the Riviera idea and for us to come up with a story that would take them down there.

"Of course when we had that discussion in 2019, before anyone had even heard of Covid, that all seemed a fantastic idea. When the pandemic kicked in and Julian and I had to stop work on another production in New York [HBO's *The Gilded Age*] and come back to the

UK, the subsequent lockdown between March and the summer of 2020 gave us the opportunity to work on the *Downton* script. At that point we thought, well, thank goodness we hadn't planned to shoot the movie until the following year, when we assumed everything would be back to normal. So we pushed on with the script, sent it out to the actors in the autumn, did deals with them, and signed them all up.

"Everything was going swimmingly until a second wave of Covid hit the UK in December 2020, by which time we were into preproduction for the film, and from then all the way to April 2021, I was incredibly concerned about new Covid variants and borders closing. What should have been a fairly simple operation logistically—and as a successful film franchise we had the budget to go to the South of France—rapidly became a pretty dicey operation during which we constantly worried about whether or not we would make it to France.

"As a result, we were forced to come up with Plan Z, a contingency plan made up of locations in Scotland and Kent that would stand in for France if we couldn't make it there. I termed it Plan Z because it was more of a last-resort, fingers-crossed-we-don't-have-to-do-it option, as we were so reliant on the weather. And the whole time we were eventually shooting in France, it rained in the UK pretty much every day, which would have been fairly disastrous for us.

"Thankfully, we managed to get everyone out there, and I followed on a few days later. On the day that the cast and crew were flying out, we had one scheduled and one charter flight taking them, and I was on such tenterhooks that I followed the flights at home on my iPad using an online flight tracker. I followed them taking off, crossing the French coastline, and it was only when they landed that I could finally breathe a sigh of relief."

GARETH NEAME • *Producer*

THE FICTIONAL WORLD OF *DOWNTON ABBEY* has now reached 1928, a year that witnessed countless important milestones in the United Kingdom, from the extension of the vote to women over the age of twenty-one to the discovery of the world's first true antibiotic, penicillin, by Scottish physician Sir Alexander Fleming. In September of that year, British audiences were also introduced to their first talking film when *The Jazz Singer* opened in London.

The latter, in particular, caught the eye of *Downton Abbey*'s creators, who have always looked to real events on which to shape storylines. The year saw a tremendous buzz among filmgoers about the first talking movies, and the industry, caught on the back foot, had to evolve rapidly to embrace the new technology. Such an occurrence is reflected in *Downton Abbey: A New Era* when a film crew move into the estate to make a silent picture and find that halfway through production they must add sound. It's a little-told part of early British cinema history, which is also personally connected to Gareth Neame, *Downton Abbey*'s producer.

The multi-award-winning producer, who conceived *Downton Abbey* with Julian Fellowes, represents the fourth generation of a family that has been blazing a trail in the film and television industry back to the silent era. Gareth's paternal great-grandmother, Ivy Close, starred in a long list of silent films

Gareth's paternal great-grandmother, Ivy Close, starred in a long list of silent films from 1914 to 1927.

from 1914 to 1927, including a lead role in French film director Abel Gance's innovative *La Roue* in 1923. Ivy's "dreamy, sylph-like brand of loveliness" had previously led to her winning the *Daily Mirror*'s Most Beautiful Woman in the World competition in 1908, during which she caught the eye of society photographer Elwin "Senny" Neame. They married, and Senny went on to try his hand in the new moving-image business, directing Ivy in several films, including *The Lady of Shalott* (1912). Four years later, Ivy crossed the pond to America, where she went on to make films in Jacksonville, Florida, working with Oliver Hardy of the Laurel and Hardy comedy duo.

Back in England, tragedy struck in 1923 when Senny was killed in a motorcycle accident. With money now tight, eldest son Ronald (Gareth's grandfather), still in his early teens, was sent out to work. He was taken on by Elstree Studios in Hertfordshire, and Gareth remembers his grandfather Ronnie telling him lots of stories about his first years there: "It was still the era of the silent movie when he arrived, and Elstree was at that point just a great big warehouse partitioned into four or five sections, each shooting a different film because they didn't have to worry about sound.

"Then, of course, when sound came along, everything changed. My grandfather remembers the cameras, which were incredibly noisy, being contained in wooden boxes to muffle their noise. And then the soundmen took over, who were very much a new breed, and the cameras were rather limited in what they could do."

At Elstree, Ronald got to work for the already renowned director Alfred Hitchcock, principally as assistant cameraman on the first British talkie, *Blackmail*, which started production in 1928 as a silent movie and then switched to sound, just as we see happen in the *Downton Abbey* movie. In fact, the making of Hitchcock's *Blackmail* inspired much of the storyline around the making of the fictional film, *The Gambler*, set at Downton Abbey. To reduce noise, the camera was placed in a large, insulated box for both movies (re-created for *A New Era* as none from the period exist), and Lady Mary provides the voice for Myrna Dalgleish, just as English actress Joan Barry did for Czech-born Anny Ondra in *Blackmail*.

Gareth's grandfather Ronnie went on to become one of the leading cinematographers in Britain, honing his craft on low-budget movies and the wildly popular comedies starring the ukulele-playing George Formby. Having collaborated with Noël Coward and David Lean on the Academy Award–nominated *In Which We Serve* (1942), Neame went on to form the production company Cineguild with Lean and Anthony Havelock-Allan. Together they produced and wrote the screenplays for two British classics, *Brief Encounter* (1945) and *Great Expectations* (1946), both of which were nominated for an Oscar for best screenplay. Neame then directed a number of films in the 1950s and 1960s, many of which featured Alec Guinness and John Mills, as well as Judy Garland's final performance in *I Could Go On Singing* (1963). In 1969, he would direct Maggie Smith—some forty years before her appearance in *Downton Abbey*—in *The Prime of Miss Jean Brodie*, for which she received an Oscar. Just a few years later, he would direct the immensely successful disaster movie *The Poseidon Adventure* (1972).

Gareth's father, Christopher, followed his father into film, working at Hammer Films in the 1960s with Peter Cushing and Christopher Lee. In the 1970s and 1980s, he would bring many of his film techniques to television, producing, among other programs, *The Flame Trees*

of Thika (1981) mini series, which starred David Robb, *Downton Abbey*'s Dr. Clarkson. He also adapted the Graham Greene novel *Monsignor Quixote* as a television movie (1985), with Alec Guinness in the leading role.

Having grown up immersed in the film business, including visiting Elstree Studios as a teen in the 1980s and even serving Brian Blessed an ice cream just before his "Gordon's alive" sequence in *Flash Gordon* (1980), it's no surprise that Gareth Neame followed in his family's footsteps. "I did feel a sense of duty in following the three generations before me, and I was lucky to form a very strong relationship with my grandfather as I got older." Sadly, Ronald Neame died in 2010 at ninety-nine on the final day of shooting of *Downton Abbey*'s first season, so he never got to see it or witness the extraordinary success of the series. He no doubt would have appreciated the passing mention in season three of his film-star mother Ivy Close, whom footman Alfred cites as one of his favorite idols on the big screen.

> *"I did feel a sense of duty following the three generations before me."*

TOP LEFT Ivy Close, winner of the *Daily Mirror*'s Most Beautiful Woman in the World competition in 1908. **TOP RIGHT** Ivy Close and the eight horsepower Rover car, presented to her by the *Daily Mirror*. **BOTTOM LEFT** Ivy Close in *La Roue*. **BOTTOM RIGHT** Gareth Neame's grandfather, producer Ronald Neame on the set of Great Expectations with director David Lean and Anthony Wager, who played Pip.

JULIAN FELLOWES • *Writer & Producer*

"YOU CAN HAVE ALL SORTS OF DISCUSSIONS, but there comes a point when you just have to pick up your pen and get on with it," says Julian Fellowes, the creative mind behind *Downton Abbey* and its extraordinary array of characters and storylines that intertwine and enthrall in equal measure. When Fellowes picks up that pen, he can conjure up just the right words for each character—provide that perfect zinger for the Dowager Countess, draw out the poignancy of a scene, push the romantic beat a little further, strike a faultless comic note—all within deftly written scripts that have earned him countless awards along the way.

In writing for the movie, Julian is building on a world he has created across six television seasons, during which we have followed around thirty key characters above and below stairs. "A long-running series gives you much more freedom and latitude to involve the audience in characters of every shape and size. And I like that—I think it's a luxury. So, for instance, you can give characters in middle age romantic or private lives in a way that would be much harder in a one-off. And for a drama series, and it can be set in any period or setting, if the public feel involved with the characters, they will follow them, and that makes for a hit show."

The attention that Julian Fellowes gives to his characters was something that also struck *A New Era*'s director, Simon Curtis. "I'm a great admirer of Chekhov, and his plays often came to mind when I was working with

"Every character is treated with great love and respect."

Julian's scripts," recalls Simon. "Every character is treated with great love and respect. Chekhov tells lots of stories for each player, and each character, whether they have a small or large part, has a narrative with a beginning, middle, and end. There's a humor and poignancy to his writing, and I was really struck by how Chekhovian Julian's writing is."

For the second movie, Julian knew he wanted to create something of a two-pronged story using events that were firmly rooted in the history of the period while also giving the characters, the servants in particular, new things to do. The trip to the French Riviera and the making of an early sound film at Downton provided just that, with some characters transported to the very different setting of the Mediterranean and the downstairs servants, dressed in Victorian finery, brought in as supporting artists for the fictional film at Downton. The film within the film, which is titled *The Gambler*, also sees new characters at Downton, principally in the form of director Jack Barber (Hugh Dancy), actor Guy Dexter (Dominic West), and actress Myrna Dalgleish (Laura Haddock).

"I thought the visiting actors did a great job," says Julian. "It's not always easy coming into a show with an established pattern and style, but they managed it really well. Whilst they might appear in quite a few scenes, only around four of those scenes will tell their particular story, whereas other scenes will focus on other storylines, and it all needs to blend

together. The established *Downton* players are used to this. They know they'll get a few scenes that tell their plot, along with supportive scenes that remind viewers of the plot and other scenes that are just life at Downton, all of which come together to tell the story. That's the style of the show."

These new characters all interact with the family and household staff: director Jack Barber works closely with and falls for Lady Mary, while screen idol Guy Dexter and Thomas Barrow develop something of a connection. "I loved the story between Thomas and Guy. It's all implied. There's never a moment when they fall into each other's arms, and yet what there is between them is perfectly clear."

Much of the filmmaking storyline is inspired by the making of Alfred Hitchcock's *Blackmail*, released in 1929. Like *The Gambler*, it had to rapidly convert to sound halfway through and involved an English actress providing the voice for the heavily accented leading lady. "By chance, Gareth Neame's grandfather worked on that movie, and when he told me what happened during its making, I thought, well that's our story!" The film stars at Downton Abbey are also inspired by real actors of the period, in particular the character of Guy Dexter, who, Julian explains, was based on Ronald Colman. "He had gone to Hollywood and established himself as a leading man in silent pictures. He was handsome, good at acting, and people liked working with him. But his real golden ticket was his beautiful voice, and when he recorded his first talking picture, producers were blown away."

While Downton is turned upside down with the making of the film, Lord and Lady Grantham and several other members of the Crawley household head off to the very different setting of the South of France, far removed from their Yorkshire estate. It's a much less formal atmosphere, where Miss Baxter and Mr. Bates can go sightseeing and conversations among some of the servants can be a little more relaxed. Away from Downton Abbey, Lord Grantham is also without his usual support system and grand surroundings, and with the unsettling news of his mother's previous liaison with the elder Marquis de Montmirail, he is having to wrestle with the fact that he may not be his father's son.

"The whole philosophical basis of the aristocracy is blood. There is nothing that is more important. He is the Earl of Grantham and if he discovers that isn't the case, even if he has the castle, land, and all the trappings that go with it, he is still nothing—he's an impostor. And that's what Robert is facing in the middle of the film, alongside the fact that his mother is dying and his wife might also be staring death in the face. He's staying in a French villa in a strange environment where he doesn't know anyone, facing the possibility that he is not the person he thought he was—and it shakes him."

OPPOSITE TOP Julian Fellowes shares a moment with Elizabeth McGovern. **OPPOSITE BOTTOM** Julian with some key cast members (left to right): Elizabeth McGovern, Michelle Dockery, Penelope Wilton, and new member Hugh Dancy. **ABOVE** Julian and Michelle Dockery on set at Highclere Castle.

LIZ TRUBRIDGE • *Producer*

"EVERY DAY I HAVE THE SAME QUESTION IN MY mind, will this work?" Producer Liz Trubridge has never taken the success of *Downton Abbey* for granted, despite having overseen all six of the phenomenally successful seasons and the first movie.

"Producing the first movie was nerve-racking, as we didn't know whether our core audience would want to go to the cinema, so it was such a thrill when big numbers of them did! The pressure now is whether we can repeat that success, and we've been very conscious all the way through that we're doing something a little different, that we're taking some of our beloved characters to a new environment, whilst also anchoring much of the movie in a world that everyone knows."

Liz was not only involved in developing the script with Julian Fellowes and Gareth Neame but

also oversaw the day-to-day filming, working closely with director Simon Curtis, co-producer Mark Hubbard, director of photography (DOP) Andrew Dunn, and the whole production crew. "I was on set next to Simon pretty much all the time. We have a very large ensemble cast and scenes with lots of people, so I'm there as an extra pair of eyes. I might spot something, such as an actor's reaction, that will need capturing, and there's constant dialogue on set."

As a producer, Liz sees herself as something of an enabler, and that means creating an environment on set that puts actors at ease, allowing them to bring their best work, while also supporting anyone who might be feeling nervous in front of the camera. "One of the great things about *Downton* is that longtime cast are very comfortable with one another and are welcoming to the new cast. I remember a few scenes with Hugh Dancy where we had to stop filming as there was so much laughter on set partly as a result of Dame Maggie making Hugh laugh so much."

The casting of new characters in *Downton*, as overseen by casting director Jill Trevellick, was made a little trickier this time round because of Covid restrictions. That meant that initial meetings were held online, and there were concerns that Hugh Dancy, who is based in the United States, wouldn't be able to make filming in the United Kingdom, though, thankfully, he managed it. A decision was made to cast a British actor in the part of Guy Dexter, a character originally conceived as an American, and Dominic West ultimately proved the perfect choice for the part.

Covid also added to the complexities and pressures of filming, and anxiety ran high over whether or not the cast and crew would make it to France. While getting there was an achievement in itself, there was also the slight worry that the director and DOP hadn't seen the house where they were planning to shoot, and those that had seen it had only done so many months earlier, Covid allowing.

Concerns, however, soon melted away when a small team of the production crew went to the villa the day after arriving in France. "We knew being there would make all the difference," explains Liz, "and of course it's all about the light and that heat, which is almost impossible to capture elsewhere,

especially in the UK, where the weather was pretty dire while we were in France.

"The principal feeling we had, however, in walking around that villa was the utter relief and sudden realization that the location was perfect. No longer would we have to run two schedules encompassing a backup plan that was, in all honesty, something of a compromise. It was the realization that we could deliver what we had dreamed for the film, and it made for a very special moment."

From right, producer Liz Trubridge, director Simon Curtis, and first assistant director, Adam Lock in the small town of Martigues, close to Marseilles in the South of France. Getting the cast and crew to the Mediterranean was touch and go during the pandemic, but they were thrilled to make it.

INSIDE DOWNTON ABBEY

Highclere Castle once again provides the glorious setting for *Downton Abbey*, a substantial Gothic edifice complete with turreted towers that was remodeled in the 1840s and is in reality the country seat of the Earls of Carnarvon. It is and always has been the main fulcrum of the series, with a varied array of state rooms and interiors decorated with family portraits, tapestries, and antiques as befits an old and noble family such as the Earls of Grantham.

For the second movie, filming took place in Highclere's great hall, where we see the now-familiar grand oak staircase overlooked by a stone gallery. The state dining room, the scene of much family drama over the years, also makes an appearance, as do the drawing room, library, and grounds of Highclere's one-hundred-acre estate.

The downstairs servants' area, including Mrs. Patmore's kitchen, the servants' hall and corridors, the servants' bedrooms, and some of the state bedrooms were built at Ealing Studios in London. Award-winning production designer Donal Woods, who has overseen the look and period feel of *Downton Abbey* since season one, jokes, "I must be the most ecological designer in the world, as that set has been rolled out for six seasons and

two films. But it always needs rebuilding and revamping, and we have added a few extra sets, such as a servery, a silver room, and even the French hat shop."

Also re-created at Ealing was the gambling club, which in *A New Era*'s storyline is based in Downton Abbey's smoking room. "We needed a lot of space for that scene, as we had to fit in a roulette table, the fictional film crew and cast, and a huge camera box, as well as our own film crew, so it was quite crowded!" The Dowager's bedroom was also built at Ealing, though as Donal explains, "We redecorated it but kept it in the colors that Violet has had from the start—mauves, light blue, purple, and gray—which fit the end of the Victorian age, rather than the bright colors of the 1920s. She has always remained in her era."

Sue Johnston plays Violet's feisty lady's maid, Denker. A headstrong and sometimes mischievous character, Denker is nonetheless fiercely protective of her mistress.

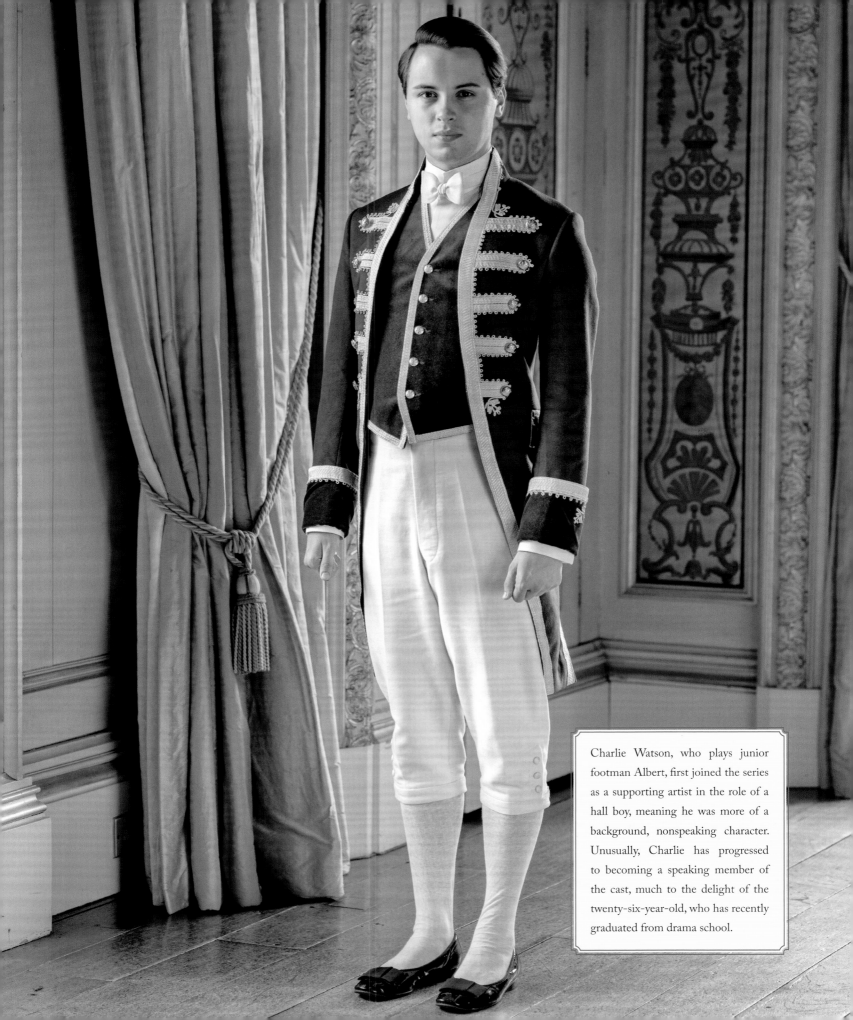

Charlie Watson, who plays junior footman Albert, first joined the series as a supporting artist in the role of a hall boy, meaning he was more of a background, nonspeaking character. Unusually, Charlie has progressed to becoming a speaking member of the cast, much to the delight of the twenty-six-year-old, who has recently graduated from drama school.

CRAWLEY FAMILY TREE

Generations of the Crawley family have lived at Downton Abbey. Five Earls of Grantham preceded Patrick Crawley, the now-deceased husband of Violet and father to Robert and Rosamund. The family tree encompasses four generations, from those who were born early in the Victorian era to the younger generation born in the 1920s, who will live out their lives in the twentieth century.

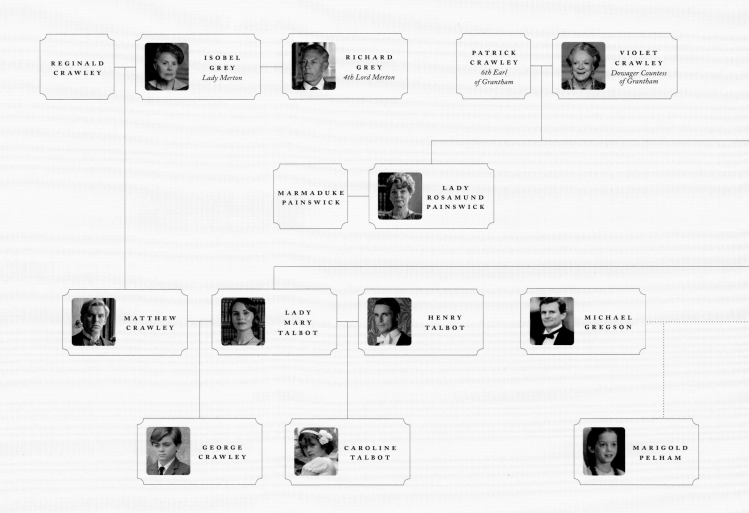

"I suppose the point is,
individual Crawleys come and go.
But the family lives on."

—CORA

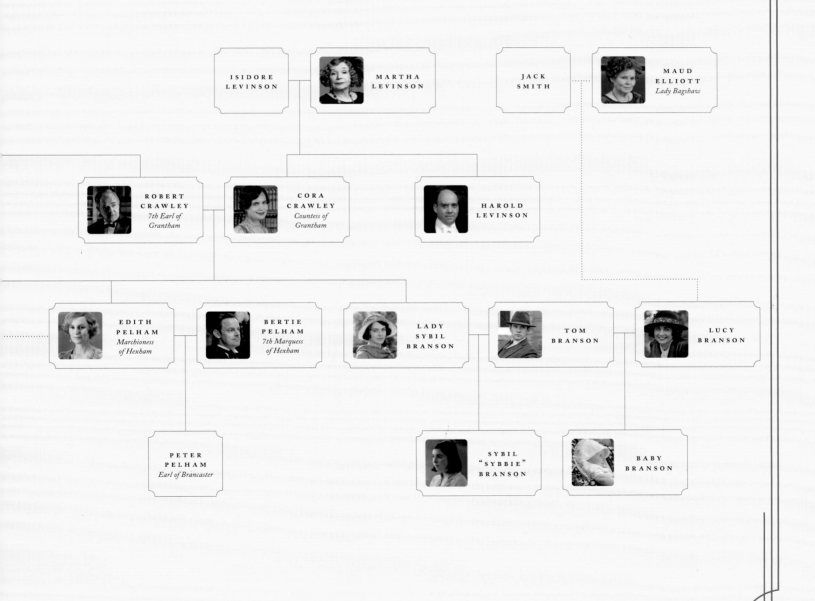

Lord Grantham's only sister, Rosamund, is played by Samantha Bond. She is a frequent visitor at Downton Abbey and has a close bond with Robert and her nieces.

DAVID ROBB
DR. CLARKSON

"*Dr. Clarkson is very much a pragmatist—he adheres to rank and position because that's how society is. It was originally envisaged that Dr. Clarkson came from Yorkshire. I suggested making him Scottish (partly because I'm half Scottish) and from Edinburgh, where, in fact, many medics graduated in the late 1890s.*"

Violet and family discuss the issue of Monsieur de Montmirail's will with family lawyer George Murray, played by Jonathan Coy. Despite having been in *Downton Abbey* since the first episode of season one, this was Jonathan's first ever scene with Dame Maggie Smith. "I was really looking forward to it, and she was absolutely delightful."

2

ROMANCES & WEDDINGS

Outside the small church of Brompton, there is an excited crowd of well-wishers and a line of chauffeured cars. Inside, the Crawley family and assembled servants of Downton Abbey look on as Lucy and Tom recite their marriage vows. The newlyweds then emerge from the church and kiss, and bridesmaids Sybbie, Marigold, and Caroline and page boy George mill around while villagers and estate staff cheer and throw rose petals over the happy couple.

It's a scene full of joy, a celebration of love, which is at the very heart of *Downton Abbey*. "All of the characters are given an opportunity to feel love," says Julian Fellowes, "to turn love down, to love the wrong person, to make a mess of it, or to make a good thing of it. But I think on the whole, love is a very key ingredient to all our lives."

Over the years, we have watched the characters of *Downton Abbey* navigate the tricky path of love, from those early stirrings of attraction and romance to the exchange of wedding vows and the ups and downs of married life, which, as Lady Mary reminds us in the movie, "is a novel, not a short story, full of plot twists along the way."

A central thread of *Downton Abbey* has always been the need for its characters to find love and happiness and to overcome the many obstacles that are invariably thrown their way. For Mary, Edith, and Sybil—who could never inherit Downton Abbey due to the primogeniture system, which recognizes only male heirs—that meant finding husbands from the rather small pool of bachelors deemed suitable for the daughters of an earl.

And for three young ladies inexperienced in matters of love and determined to live their own lives that naturally proved a difficult ask. Thankfully, they all eventually found love— even Sybil before her life was tragically cut short. But along the way, they sometimes made a mess of things as they went through the gut-wrenching lows and giddy highs of romance and occasionally skated on very thin ice when it came to avoiding scandal.

For the servants downstairs, long working hours mean they have less time or opportunity to find suitors, though there has always been a regular influx of new maids, hall boys, or tradesmen to catch someone's eye and add a bit of romantic interest. In many houses of the period, female employees who did marry would often leave service, which is why Mrs. Patmore and Mrs. Hughes were unmarried well into middle age (the "Mrs." was a courtesy title given to housekeepers and cooks). In addition to all sorts of practicalities that hinder the path of romance, there are universal forces at play that affect both the upstairs and downstairs worlds: misplaced loyalties, the inability of some characters to express or acknowledge how they feel, foolish pride, and miscommunication of various forms.

Against all these odds, however, many of the characters in *Downton Abbey* succeed in finding love, and we share in the relief and utter joy when they finally summon up the courage to propose or declare their love. Who can forget Matthew Crawley on a snowy night on bended knee in front of Lady Mary; Anna announcing, "I love you, Mr. Bates"; or Mr. Carson's endearingly clumsy confession to Mrs Hughes, "I do want to be stuck with you," to which Mrs. Hughes answers, "Of course I'll marry you, you old booby!" The words and actions might be simple or even blundering, but the passions behind them are heartfelt and very real.

So far, *Downton* has featured eight wedding ceremonies, which include the grand society wedding of Matthew and Mary and her subsequent, more understated but no-less-touching nuptials with Henry Talbot. We saw Edith finally make it down the aisle only to suffer the indignity of being abandoned at the altar, though she would later secure herself a far better prize in the form of Bertie Pelham (who later became Lord Hexham). The hastily arranged bedside ceremony between Daisy and William Mason on his flower-strewn deathbed made for a moving scene, as did the simple registry ceremony between Anna and Mr. Bates and the very sweet and unfussy wedding of Mr. Carson and Mrs. Hughes, arranged exactly to the head housekeeper's wishes.

> *"Of course I'll marry you,*
> *you old booby!"*
>
> **—MRS. HUGHES**

Over the years, we've also seen numerous examples of love that is forbidden or deemed unacceptable. Thomas, whose homosexuality brings him to the brink of despair, is forced either to suppress or hide his sexuality, always with the threat of a prison sentence over his head. Lady Sybil shocked the family when she ran away to marry the family chauffeur, Tom Branson. Lady Rose's marriage to a Jewish banking heir caused Lord Merton's sons to cast aspersions, and we discover that in her youth even the Dowager Countess had romantic affairs with foreign noblemen, which perhaps goes some way to explain her quip, "One way or another, everyone goes down the aisle with half the story hidden."

What is also a delight in *Downton Abbey* are the romances that blossom between older cast members. Lord Merton's proposal to Isobel Crawley was unutterably pleasing, and even Mrs. Patmore experiences something of a romance with Mr. Mason, characters who might not be expecting romance at their time of life but are nonetheless just as in need of love and companionship. Characters are also given second (or multiple) chances when it comes to finding love: Lady Mary isn't doomed to spinsterhood after an unfortunate sexual liaison with the Turkish dignitary Kemal Pamuk; Lady Edith battles on despite often being overlooked as the middle daughter, marrying a veritable grandee who welcomes her illegitimate daughter; and even Tom Branson, who tragically lost his first love, Lady Sybil, unexpectedly finds love again with Lucy Smith, who was once the "secret" daughter of Lady Bagshaw but is now the radiant bride of Brompton Park.

TOM & LUCY BRANSON

Allen Leech & Tuppence Middleton

Tom and Lucy deserve their happiness, and their wedding symbolizes the coming together of the two worlds of *Downton*, both characters having entered the aristocratic world by irregular means.

Irish-born Tom Branson, played by Allen Leech, first arrived at Downton as the family chauffeur and caused outrage when he and Sybil, the youngest daughter of Robert and Cora, fell in love and ended up eloping to Ireland with only Mary and Edith present at their simple ceremony. The couple returned to Downton when Sybil fell pregnant, where she sadly died giving birth to their daughter, also named Sybil (but known as Sybbie). Tom, like the rest of the family, mourned the loss of his wife deeply and, after a brief period away, returned to Downton with Sybbie. No longer the strident socialist he once was, Tom has learned to live happily at the estate, though he is still sometimes baffled by the ways of the landed classes and is keen that his own family doesn't become part of the "idle rich."

Lucy Smith, played by Tuppence Middleton, first visited Downton Abbey as maid to Lady Bagshaw (played by Imelda Staunton), a distant relative of the Crawleys. It was soon revealed that Lucy was in fact the illegitimate daughter of Lady Bagshaw, the product of a liaison with her deceased husband's army servant, Jack Smith. Tom and Lucy were instantly attracted to each other, aided by the fact that they had both experienced a rise in social status, Tom now as an established member of the Crawley family and Lucy as heir to the Brompton estate.

The two share a romantic moment in the film as they swim in the waters of the Mediterranean, Tom confessing to Lucy, "I love you, you know. In a way I thought I'd never love again." Thanks to Violet, Tom's daughter, Sybbie, will inherit Villa des Colombes in the South of France. Tom wrestles with the fact that it's not a working estate, whereas Lucy can see the villa will make a wonderful place for the family to get together in the summer. They are blissfully happy and even more so when they learn Lucy is pregnant: love and life have prevailed, and their child marks the next stage in the *Downton* story.

LORD & LADY GRANTHAM

Hugh Bonneville & Elizabeth McGovern

The central marriage of *Downton Abbey* is that of Robert and Cora, Lord and Lady Grantham, played by Hugh Bonneville and Elizabeth McGovern. Their marriage forms the solid basis on which the entire series is based, their bond strengthened by the shared love for their daughters and sense of duty to the wider family and estate.

In *A New Era*, Robert must face multiple challenges, as Hugh Bonneville explains: "The crisis at the heart of the film—for Robert at least—is that he is going to lose the three most important things in his life: his mother, his name, and his wife. He leaves for France knowing that his mother is gravely ill, before then learning he might not be the Earl of Grantham. So when Cora tells him she too is unwell, it takes him completely by surprise, and there's a sudden outpouring of emotion. Everything has been piling up, and he feels he's losing his whole world."

During the film, there is also a reminder that their marriage was initially one of convenience. Cora, like many American heiresses of the time, provided the funds the Downton estate desperately needed, and while she loved Robert from the outset, Robert's love for her, as he's rather ashamed to admit, came later but deepened over the years. He is now terrified of losing her, plaintively declaring, "You have been everything to me. Everything."

While there is undoubted love between Robert and Cora, they have faced plenty of challenges as husband and wife. For Cora, the first few years must have been particularly demanding: living in a strange land with an array of confusing customs and social niceties to master, not to mention a fierce mother-in-law to contend with. The biggest test for their marriage came when their youngest daughter, Sybil, shockingly died during childbirth, and Cora initially blamed Robert for not heeding Dr. Clarkson's warnings.

Like all couples, they also have their differences. Cora is better able to embrace change and the more modern outlook their daughters favor. Robert prefers the status quo, but with the help of his wife, he increasingly respects his daughters' choices, even if they don't quite fit with his more traditional views.

Cora and Robert discuss the recent news about Violet's inheritance of a French villa. Robert is keen to visit, as "it would mean we'd miss the whole of Mary's frightful film."

LADY MARY & HENRY TALBOT

Michelle Dockery & Matthew Goode

Lady Mary attends Tom and Lucy's wedding without her own husband, Henry Talbot, who is abroad, as she puts it, at a "barmy" car rally. Having married just three years earlier, they are still very much in love, though Mary is a little downhearted that she is not always at the top of her husband's list of priorities.

"He's in love with cars. He's in love with speed. He's in love with adventure," she confesses to Edith. "He's also in love with me, I think, but I don't seem to cancel out the other three."

They have two children, Caroline, who is two, and George, the now seven-year-old son from Mary's first marriage to Matthew Crawley, who died in a car accident the day of George's birth. Lady Mary's first wedding was a grand affair, and her memories of Matthew are that he was "perfect, really. As handsome as a prince in a fairy tale, moral, strong, full of dreams, determined to do his bit." For that reason, it took Mary a long time to get over losing Matthew and eventually find love with handsome racing car driver Henry Talbot, whom she describes as "much more pragmatic . . . he's a do-er," though he is clearly the right match for Mary.

Over the years, Mary's natural beauty, aristocratic poise, and sharp intelligence have attracted many suitors, though she has made mistakes along the way. Long before Matthew, duty rather than love dictated her brief unofficial engagement to Downton heir Patrick Crawley, and her subsequent engagement with the ruthless newspaper proprietor Richard Carlisle—principally so Mary could avoid a scandal over a former sexual encounter with Turkish dignitary Kemal Pamuk—was similarly short-lived. Years later, Mary became involved with family friend Anthony Foyle, Lord Gillingham, though she turned down his proposal as she was still grieving the loss of her first husband.

In the movie, film director Jack Barber works closely with Lady Mary and becomes strongly attracted to her. She is flattered by his attentions—"Nothing is nicer for an old married woman than to find she's still an object of desire"—and is tempted to kiss him. But she soon shakes off the desire, observing, "I'm too old-fashioned to believe that what I want is the only thing that matters." Her allegiance is to her husband and to the Downton estate that she now runs, and no one—not even Jack Barber—is going to get in the way of that.

LORD & LADY HEXHAM

Harry Hadden-Paton & Laura Carmichael

Over the years, Lady Edith, played by Laura Carmichael, has suffered more than her fair share of bad luck when it has come to romance. Unrequited love for her cousin Patrick Crawley was followed by an engagement to the considerably older Sir Anthony Strallan, who subsequently abandoned her at the altar.

An affair with her employer and publisher Michael Gregson led to her becoming pregnant with Marigold, only for him to disappear and eventually be killed in Germany. It's an unfortunate train of events for "poor Edith," once deemed the overlooked middle sister who lacked the advantages of her siblings.

All that bad luck would eventually end when she met the very eligible and thoroughly decent Bertie Pelham (who later became Lord Hexham). A little wobble ensued when Edith tried to conceal Marigold's identity, but Bertie forgave her and welcomed Edith and Marigold to the family seat of Brancaster Castle, the couple marrying on New Year's Eve at the end of season six. As Marquess and Marchioness of Hexham, the couple now outrank in nobility the Crawleys, much to the initial annoyance of Edith's older sister, Mary.

Beginning in childhood, the two sisters have had considerable rivalry and tend to bring out the very worst in each other.

Since the last movie, Bertie and Edith have welcomed baby Peter. As he is being looked after by a nanny at Brancaster Castle, they decide to leave Marigold at Downton and join the family on their jaunt to France. Having returned to work on a part-time basis, Edith wants to write an article about the trend for people to visit the South of France in the summer. Bertie, along with Cora, is encouraging of Edith's career and can see how happy it makes her.

"Bertie is completely smitten with his wife," explains Harry Hadden-Paton, who plays Bertie. "He's very supportive of her, and they're a happy couple. Everything has worked out for Edith, and that gives viewers such satisfaction."

MR. CARSON & MRS. HUGHES

Jim Carter & Phyllis Logan

Mr. Carson and Mrs. Hughes are another relatively recently married couple, following a courtship that Jim Carter describes as "the longest-burning, slowest romance in the history of television."

The creators behind *Downton Abbey* admit they had no plans to bring the couple together at the beginning of the series, but they make such a wonderful duo—Mrs. Hughes's wise and pragmatic nature providing the perfect foil to Mr. Carson's more conservative tendencies—that it seemed natural for something of a romance to develop.

When Mr. Carson finally made his feelings for Mrs. Hughes clear, they agreed to marry in season six and said their I do's in front of the whole village, followed by a reception in the schoolhouse. Three years later, and in the cottage they now share on the grounds of the estate, Mr. Carson voices his horror over the news of "moving picture" people arriving at Downton. Lady Mary and Mrs. Hughes are equally horrified at the thought of Carson keeping watch over them, so Mrs. Hughes masterfully convinces her husband that he should travel with the family to France so he can "show them how things should be managed." Carson agrees and takes to his mission with gusto.

On their return, and satisfied that he has shown the French what it is to deal with an English butler, Carson is shaken by the news that Violet is sinking fast, though still mortified that "so great a lady should go when the house is full of *film people*." He later agrees to return to Downton Abbey from retirement to help break in the new butler now that Barrow is leaving. When Mary confesses that she's a little frightened at having the "Downton torch" passed to her, Mr. Carson assures her she has the strength required, a poignant scene that reflects the endearing bond between the two and that shows a more tender side of Mr. Carson. "In the same way, Mary does on occasion show a vulnerability with me—more so sometimes than with her father, Lord Grantham," suggests Jim, "and Carson can boost her resolve or at least emphasize that she always has his support."

Of course, Mr. Carson, with his steadfast loyalty to the Crawley family, needs no convincing to return to Downton to run the household, at least in the short term, alongside head housekeeper and his doughty wife, Mrs. Hughes.

While Mrs. Hughes is often a little snippy with Mr. Carson, she has a good heart and there is a real tenderness between the couple. They have had their ups and downs but have always had great respect and fondness for each other.

Mr. Carson, played by Jim Carter, is somewhat embarrassed when a French shopkeeper assumes he and Maud Bagshaw (Imelda Staunton) are husband and wife. In reality, the two actors are married, and the scene provided the two characters, "who haven't had much to do with each other until now," a cheeky excuse to play alongside each other.

LORD & LADY MERTON

Douglas Reith & Penelope Wilton

Lord and Lady Merton are still "wildly in love," as Douglas Reith puts it, the actor who plays Lord Merton. "She is everything that my former wife, Ada, was not. I had a miserable life with Ada and my two sons, Larry in particular."

Lord Merton and Isobel Crawley, played by Penelope Wilton, married in 1925, after an on-again, off-again courtship during which Lord Merton did his best to woo Isobel. His two sons and daughter-in-law, Amelia, did their best to derail the union, having deemed middle-class Isobel below their status. Audiences around the world willed Isobel to accept Lord Merton's tender marriage proposal: "I state freely and proudly Isobel that I have fallen in love with you and I want to spend what remains of my life in your company. I believe I could make you happy." Fortunately, Lord Merton was right, and their subsequent marriage seems as happy and harmonious as any could hope.

Isobel, of course, deserves happiness, having lost her first husband, Dr. Reginald Crawley, and only son, Matthew, shortly after Lady Mary gave birth to her grandson, George. A trained nurse, Isobel is pragmatic,

principled, and unafraid to voice views that might clash with the aristocratic views around her (primarily those of Violet). Lord Merton, who is an old family friend of the Crawleys and godfather to Lady Mary, is from a distinctly aristocratic background, but, like Isobel, he is forward thinking and sympathetic to his second wife's more progressive views.

From the outset, plain-speaking Isobel clashed with uncompromising Violet, though their relationship evolved into friendship and mutual respect, so much so that Violet, in her final days, entrusts Isobel to go through her private letters. Isobel, like Violet, has softened toward her former adversary, with whom she has exchanged countless verbal slights over the years, the two a formidable match for each other. Isobel will keenly miss Violet, agreeing with Cora that life will be strange without her. "I shall miss having a sparring partner to keep me trim."

PENELOPE WILTON
LADY MERTON

Penelope Wilton was delighted when Isobel finally married Lord Merton. "He seemed to be a rather forward-looking man from Isobel's point of view, and he was honest and sweet. He was truly fond of her and loved her, and she grew to love him very much."

MRS. PATMORE & MR. MASON

Lesley Nicol & Paul Copley

Mrs. Patmore, cook and formidable presence in the kitchen of Downton Abbey, has had little in the way of romance in her life. "A lady of that age, from that background and place in life," muses Lesley Nicol, who plays Mrs. Patmore, "would think any kind of romance developing very unlikely.

But at the same time, we're all human, we all have feelings, and I believe when she met Mr. Mason, she just took a shine to him, and he was the same with her. And they've always got on incredibly well."

Mr. Mason is a tenant farmer on the Downton estate and father to the late William Mason, who ten years earlier was briefly married to kitchen maid Daisy just before he died. Mr. Mason now shares his home with newlyweds Daisy and Andy, though it's clear three's a crowd, and the arrangement isn't working. When it becomes apparent that Mr. Mason and Mrs. Patmore are fond of each other, Mrs. Patmore even admitting that she was sweet on him "about a hundred years ago," she and Daisy set about persuading Mr. Mason to consider moving into Mrs. Patmore's cottage so the young couple can have more space to themselves.

Mrs. Patmore achieves this by plying an already-giddy Mr. Mason with red wine when they're playing the part of extras in the dining room film scene, as Paul Copley, who plays Mr. Mason, explains: "Mrs. Patmore has, over the years, provided Mr. Mason with sweet treats and bakes, meat and veg—food and drink, it's what she knows!" While Mrs. Patmore is often shown barking orders in the kitchen, Lesley likes how Julian Fellowes in the writing always shows a different side to his characters: "Mrs. Patmore is not just a grumpy cook. She has a little dalliance that makes her go a bit aflutter. It's obvious she and Mr. Mason have a liking for each other, and I think she can't quite believe it when he agrees to move in with her!"

DAISY & ANDY

Sophie McShera & Michael Fox

Assistant cook Daisy has always been something of a romantic, though she had a habit of falling for the wrong type, from Thomas Barrow (even though Mrs. Patmore valiantly tried to explain to Daisy that he was "not a ladies' man") to footman-turned-valet Alfred, whose head was already turned by kitchen maid Ivy.

Daisy has also had her fair share of admirers, including Mr. Mason's son, William, whom (a little reluctantly) she married just hours before he died; American valet Ethan; and her now-husband, under footman Andy Parker.

There is more to Daisy, however, than romance, and over the years we've watched her mature, question what she sees around her, and form her own views about what she wants in life. It's a journey that Sophie McShera, who plays Daisy, has enjoyed: "She began as a young kitchen maid terrified of everyone and is now a woman who is not afraid to speak her mind, desires and ambitions, and political opinions." Daisy does dream of a life outside service, and for that reason, she once worried that Andy was a bit too "safe and ordinary." Having proved himself a little more passionate than he might look, Daisy agreed to push ahead with the wedding, which we learn wasn't as "grand" as Tom and Lucy's but was nonetheless "lovely."

The newlyweds now live with Mr. Mason at Yew Tree Farm, though it's not a happy arrangement, especially when it comes to Mr. Mason's punctiliousness over items in the house, driving Daisy to complain, "Mr. Mason is driving me mad. Every cup and saucer has to be right." Eventually she and Mrs. Patmore cook up a plan to convince Mr. Mason to move in with the Downton cook.

Daisy is more excited by the arrival of her film idols at Downton than she has ever been by the usual visiting grandees, including the recent visit by the king and queen. She is initially in awe of Myrna Dalgleish, until she learns they are from a similar background. She then even admonishes her for her rudeness to the servants and to put aside her worries over filming: "You're one of us, not one of them. Just remember it. Now, chop, chop, straighten your hair, and let's get going!"

Daisy and Andy, now Mr. and Mrs. Parker, look forward to spending time in the farmhouse without Mr. Mason fussing over everything.

MISS BAXTER & MR. MOLESLEY

Raquel Cassidy & Kevin Doyle

There's always been something of an understanding between Miss Baxter, lady's maid to Cora, and Mr. Molesley, schoolteacher and occasional Downton footman. They have supported each other during difficult times, and they—and it would seem the entire household—are aware of the connection between them.

In France, Miss Baxter openly admits that "her affections are very firmly engaged" to Molesley, though that doesn't stop her from enjoying the trip. "Miss Baxter really wants to go to France—she'd love to travel the world," explains Raquel Cassidy, who plays Baxter. "She's also proud about the work she does, but Mr. Molesley is in her heart."

Back at Downton, Mr. Molesley's attention is taken up with the goings-on of the movie production. We discover he's a lover of films and enthusiastically offers to help sketch out scenes and write the much-needed dialogue for the movie. He even comes up with a better ending for the film, much to the astonishment of Jack Barber and Lady Mary, who agrees "we weren't aware of his hidden talents."

"The one thing I've learned about Mr. Molesley over the years," says Kevin Doyle, the actor behind Molesley, "is that whenever he takes something on, he approaches it with great fervor, whether it's educating other people or playing cricket! And it's the same here—he just goes for it. Earlier in the series, he confessed to his father that he felt he had missed certain opportunities in life. As a result, there has always been a sense of melancholy with Molesley, mixed in with a bit of humor and pathos."

The sense of missed opportunities, however, evaporates the second that Jack Barber offers Molesley scriptwriting work and a salary far beyond that of a schoolmaster. And yet his first thought is not to go to his typewriter but to Miss Baxter and, much to the relief of everyone at Downton (who can hear through the microphones), he proposes, and she happily accepts, exclaiming, "Yes, I jolly well will, Mr. Molesley!"

The next time we see the pair is at the Dowager Countess's funeral. "It was, of course, a somber occasion," says Raquel, "but there we are, finally together and walking hand in hand, and it was all I could do not to skip and beam from ear to ear!"

ANNA & MR. BATES

Joanne Froggatt & Brendan Coyle

Valet Mr. Bates must leave his wife, Anna, and son, Johnny, when he heads off to the South of France. Lady's maid Anna, however, is excited by the presence of film stars at Downton, though Mr. Bates gently warns her not to set her expectations too high.

"We played with the notion that Anna was trying to make me jealous," explains Brendan Coyle, who plays Mr. Bates, "but we have a bit of a laugh. It's more playful than anything."

Over the years, Anna, played by Joanne Froggatt, and Mr. Bates have suffered considerable adversity leading up to and beyond their secret marriage: Mr. Bates had an unhappy first marriage, both would be sent to prison, and Anna was sexually assaulted. In the face of such bad fortune, they have remained decent, kind, and dignified people, though Mr. Bates has always been a little more reserved than his wife. "When I first took on the role," says Brendan, "I reflected on men of that generation, and I thought of my Irish and Scottish grandfathers. They were both steelworkers and dignified men, quite dapper at the weekend but not emotionally expressive or given to histrionics, and it seemed to me that was the kind of man Bates was."

Mr. Bates walks with a cane as a result of an old wound suffered during the Boer War, when he served as Lord Grantham's batman. Bates is in fact the very first character we see in the TV show: episode one features him heading toward Downton on a steam train. Some of the downstairs staff are initially unkind to him, but Anna offers him friendship and support, and the two embark on something of a slow-burn romance. As Brendan puts it, "Much of that developing romance was made up of gentle gestures and subtle moments, such as Anna simply handing Mr. Bates a cup of tea when he's not feeling well, and I think the audience responded to that. I loved the way the relationship formed and the time it took—it was allowed to breathe, which of course you can do with a long-running series."

Now that Mr. Bates and Anna have finally taken charge of their lives, it seems that, finally, they have a very happy future ahead of them.

A FRIENDLY, FAMILY WEDDING

Belchamp Hall, tucked away in rural Suffolk, provided the perfect setting for the wedding scene of Tom and Lucy that opens the film. Flowers adorn the small church situated next to a Queen Anne–style house, in front of which wedding guests mill around on a lawn dotted with colorful umbrellas and tables and a marquee strewn with bunting.

"We wanted to give the feel of a friendly, family wedding," explains production designer Donal Woods, who oversees the general look and period feel of *Downton Abbey*. "We went for soft, peachy colors and creams, with bunting and flowers—nothing dominates too much and everything is easy on the eye. It's the opening of the film, and we wanted the audience to think, oh, okay, I feel good now."

Finding the house that would stand in for Brompton Park proved challenging for the production team. They knew they wanted a beautiful house that wasn't as large as Highclere, was next to a church, and was within large grounds. "We looked at five or six houses around the UK," remembers Mark "Sparky" Ellis, the supervising location manager for *Downton Abbey*, "but as soon as we saw Belchamp Hall, everyone knew that it was the one."

When shooting on location, the mobile village that comes with every *Downton Abbey* production is big, though keeping everyone safe during the Covid pandemic added to both the scale and complexity of filming. On top of the usual cast and crew, the wedding scene included 180 extras, all of whom required costume and makeup. "We had two huge marquees set up at the back of the house, leaving the front of the house completely clear for the sweeping shot you see at the beginning of the film," explains Sparky. "But we needed an area for the generators, lighting, catering, toilets—the lot. It's all vast, and we had to be close by, as we couldn't use minibuses because of Covid restrictions. Everywhere we filmed, instead of setting up in trucks or a nearby village hall, for instance, we had marquees, which were in big demand during the pandemic!"

THE
WEDDING DRESS

As costume designer Anna Robbins recalls: "It's always a privilege to design a wedding dress for *Downton,* and you want every dress to be different and to suit the character. Tom and Lucy's wedding had a relaxed and fresh vibe to it, not so much a traditional aristocratic wedding. I wanted Lucy to feel she could pick up her skirt and have a real dance.

"I had an idea of a dress using satin, chiffon, and tulle—layers and layers of gathered silk tulle for the dropped waisted skirt so that it had a dramatic silhouette but also a light frothiness to it, cut higher at the front and into a train at the back, which was very on point for the late 1920s. I found a long vintage cape made of silver embroidered tulle, and we used that as an overlay for the satin bodice, giving the dress an amazing texture.

"The dress has a low back, which is quite daring but still pretty. I knew the first shot of the movie would go over the church and then head up the aisle where Lucy is standing before she turns round, so I wanted the back to have real drama. The veil is a hand-embroidered replica of a beautiful original and quite decorative."

Anna Robbins' original sketch for the front and back design of Lucy's beautifully layered wedding dress.

ANNA ROBBINS
COSTUME DESIGNER

"Lucy is also wearing a tiara, which would have been the first time she could as a married woman. It's likely it would have been a family heirloom passed down to her from Lady Bagshaw and would represent her entrance into a very different world. The beautiful diamond and pearl tiara was loaned to us by Bentley & Skinner of Piccadilly, London. She also wears a diamond-encrusted bow just above her heart, also from Bentley & Skinner. I wanted to pull out all the stops when it came to her jewelry."

ANNA ROBBINS
COSTUME DESIGNER

*"There was more of a
relaxed feel at the reception,
so we changed Lucy's
headdress from a tiara to
a diamanté Juliet cap."*

ANNA ROBBINS
COSTUME DESIGNER

"The men wore morning dress with pale gray waistcoats paired with gray Ascot ties, and we accessorized them with small buttonholes that were fitting for the aristocracy in this period."

3

The French Riviera

The day after Tom and Lucy's wedding, Violet announces to the family that she has come into possession of a villa in the South of France called Villa des Colombes (Villa of the Doves). It had belonged to the Marquis de Montmirail, who had bequeathed it to Violet after an "idyllic interlude" spent with her decades earlier. Following his death, his son, the current marquis, has invited the Crawleys to visit and extends the invitation to Tom and Lucy when they learn eight-year-old Sybbie will one day take ownership of the villa.

Robert and Cora agree to go, if only so they miss "the whole of Mary's frightful film," as Robert puts it. Many in the party, however, are excited to go, and it's the first time we see members of the Downton Abbey household heading abroad en masse. Miss Baxter and Mr. Bates join the group, as does Mr. Carson, having been convinced by Mrs. Hughes that only he can ensure everything will be done properly for Lord Grantham. Lady Bagshaw joins them, as she is staying with Lucy and Tom until her house is ready, and Lady Edith and Bertie also ask to accompany the party on the family adventure.

The Marquis de Montmirail (right) welcomes Lord Grantham to the Villa des Colombes.

A PARADISE OF NATURE

The destination for this small band of intrepid travelers is Toulon, situated on the Mediterranean coast in the southeast corner of France. Extending northeast from Toulon to the France-Italy border is the French Riviera or Côte d'Azur, a famous seaside stretch that includes the now-glamorous resorts of Saint-Tropez, Antibes, Cannes, and Nice. The British upper classes had been traveling to the area since the late 1700s, lured by its warm, dry climate and stunning scenery.

As Lord Grantham mentions in the movie, former statesman Lord Brougham popularized the French Riviera when he traveled there in 1834 hoping to find a cure for one of his daughters, who was suffering from tuberculosis. For some decades, the Mediterranean coast had been viewed as something of a winter health resort, and the ailing British elite flocked to the area, with French historian Paul Gonnet writing that in winter Nice filled with "a colony of pale and listless women and listless sons of nobility near death." A cholera outbreak in Nice forced Lord Brougham to stop in the then small fishing village of Cannes. So enchanted was he by its climate, light, and cuisine that he decided to buy a piece of land overlooking the sea and build his villa there, which he named after his daughter Eleonore-Louise, who died in 1839.

In his wake, other well-heeled British and members of the aristocracy sailed to the area and built their own grand villas so they too might enjoy the winter warmth. The subsequent flood of British tourists to Nice led to the naming of the seven-kilometer seafront esplanade the Promenade des Anglais. The arrival of the railway from the mid-1800s onward, along with the building of grand hotels and casinos, soon turned the area into the playground of the rich and powerful, and the coastline became the talk of Europe.

European royalty would be similarly attracted to the region, and Alexander II of Russia, Leopold II of Belgium, and the Prince of Wales (the future Edward VII) regularly traveled to Cannes. Queen Victoria was also a frequent winter visitor, holidaying no less than nine times in the area. Encouraged by British doctor James Henry Bennet, who had long been promoting the French climate as a health cure-all, Queen Victoria stayed first in Menton in 1882 and then in Cannes, Grasse, and Hyères. Her final five visits, beginning in 1895, were to Cimiez, above Nice, holidaying first at the Grand Hôtel and later at the Excelsior Hôtel Regina, where she and her staff of one hundred would take over an entire wing. So rejuvenated was she from her visits to the "paradise of nature," as she called the area, that when dying in 1901, she uttered, "Oh, if only I were at Nice, I should recover."

ABOVE Queen Victoria at Edward Cazalet's villa in Cimiez in the South of France in 1885. The queen would frequently ride out in a carriage or a cart pulled by a donkey. **OPPOSITE** The English travelers are elegantly dressed for the French Riviera.

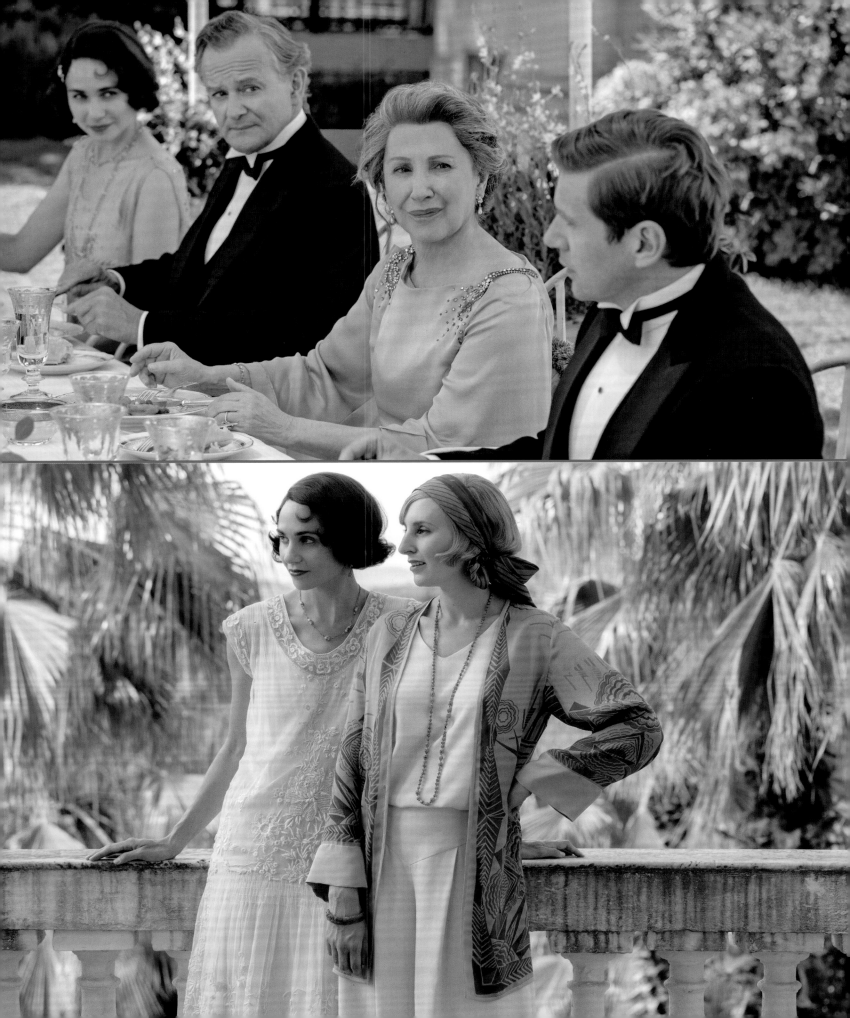

Gerald Murphy with wife Sara at the beach of Antibes (left); Beatrice Lillie and Noël Coward on holiday.

A SUNNY PLACE FOR SHADY PEOPLE

By the end of the nineteenth century, the pure light and mild climate of the French Riviera had also lured painters to the region, including Henri Matisse and Auguste Renoir, and American literati, with Henry James setting his 1903 novel *The Ambassadors* partly on the Riviera.

By the time the Downton Abbey household heads to the Riviera, some of the older members of the family assume that the French villa would only be used in the winter months. Edith tells them that people have started visiting the region in the summer months, a practice that began in the 1920s and which Edith intends to write about in an article. Gerald and Sara Murphy, a wealthy American couple, were instrumental in kickstarting the trend when they visited the area in 1923 and persuaded the owner of the Hôtel du Cap in Antibes to keep a wing of the hotel open during the summer. And when French designer Coco Chanel returned to Paris in the same year bronzed by a summer in Antibes, she inadvertently sparked a craze for tanning. By 1925, the Murphys were living in an art deco villa (Villa America) and welcoming a steady stream of artists, authors, and cultural figures, among them Ernest Hemingway, Gertrude Stein, Cole Porter, and Rudolph Valentino.

Another of the Murphys' guests was US author F. Scott Fitzgerald, who based his lead characters in *Tender Is the Night* on the couple. He began the novel in 1925 when he and his wife, Zelda, were soaking up the sun along the Cap d'Antibes, and the book captures the heady atmosphere of the 1920s Jazz Age on the Riviera. In *A New Era*, Guy Dexter paints a similar picture when he describes being "marooned on the roof of the Negresco" (a grand hotel on the Promenade des Anglais in Nice) as part of an elaborate cocktail-fueled party game, with real-life actors Ronald Colman and Gloria Swanson.

English writer Somerset Maugham, who resided off and on at Cap Ferrat from 1927 until his death, coined the description of the area as "a sunny place for shady people." A steady stream of luminaries visited Maugham at his villa in Cap Ferrat, from Picasso and Harpo Marx to Ian Fleming and even the Duke and Duchess of Windsor following the 1936 abdication of the former Edward VIII. As Maugham wrote, "The shores of the Mediterranean were littered with royalties, lured by the climate, or in exile, or escaping a scandalous past or unsuitable marriage."

LOCATIONS IN FRANCE & PLAN Z

Just as the party from Downton Abbey arrived en masse in the South of France, so too did the cast and crew for the movie. The logistics were complex, as was the scouting for locations in the face of potential travel restrictions during the Covid pandemic. Key to this was finding the perfect setting for the villa of the Marquis de Montmirail.

They were searching for one that overlooked the Mediterranean and provided just the right look and feel for the period and storyline.

"The brief I got," explains production designer Donal Woods, "was to make France totally different from anything you've ever seen in *Downton*. And we found a stunning French property, Villa Rocabella in Le Pradet near Toulon, which fit the bill perfectly. There is some traditional furniture in the house, which is apt because in the film it's owned by Madame de Montmirail, but the house itself has color, light, and is almost all open plan, with twentieth-century art and a modernity that you wouldn't have seen in Britain in 1928.

"It's all about that Mediterranean light, and because the family are in the South of France, there's a slightly less-ordered formality at dinner, more of a Scott Fitzgerald–bohemian look and a freer style which you get with that location and time in history. We've never really gone abroad in *Downton Abbey*, so if you've been a fan of all six seasons and loved the last film, this might provide something intriguing and different, and something of a visual feast."

Other locations used in France include the streets and waterfront of the port of Martigues, west of Marseilles, and the beachfront of Villa Rocabella. Fortunately, the cast and crew were able to travel to France, but the production team had up their sleeve various contingency plans, known as Plan Z, should Covid restrictions have prevented travel abroad. This involved penciling in locations around the United Kingdom that would have stood in for France, a couple of which were in Scotland near where the team filmed on the Royal Yacht *Britannia*, which carried the Queen, other members of the royal family, and official guests around the globe for more than forty years, until it was retired from service in 1997.

DOWNTON ABBEY 2 —
ARRIVAL — VILLA DES COLOMBES — FRANCE —

— CONCEPT —   VILLA DES COLOMBES — TERRACE
DOWNTON ABBEY 2

Concept sketches by production designer, Donal Woods

Despite the production team and cast being able to decamp to France, a couple of United Kingdom locations stood in for French scenes. These included the party held by the Marquis de Montmirail on the terrace of Villa des Colombes, which was shot at the orangery at Wrest Park in Bedfordshire, and the interior of the hat shop near Toulon, which was built as a set at Ealing Studios.

MARQUIS DE MONTMIRAIL

Jonathan Zaccaï

The Marquis de Montmirail invites the Downton Abbey household to the Villa des Colombes, insisting that they stay at the property. Less welcoming is his mother, Madame de Montmirail, who is clearly aggrieved that Violet, and in turn Sybbie, will inherit the holiday villa.

The current marquis is played by Belgian actor and longtime Parisian resident Jonathan Zaccaï. The French-speaking film actor was given a warm welcome by the *Downton* cast and crew, and although he enjoyed being part of their Mediterranean adventure, he admitted his English needed a little "waking up" to play the part.

Jonathan was also delighted to be playing the son of Madame de Montmirail, portrayed by esteemed French actress Nathalie Baye. While most of their scenes were shot in France, Jonathan and Nathalie were required to travel to England to film the villa party scene, which involved not only a train journey from Paris to London but also, in line with Covid and insurance regulations, a period of quarantine. "We were together in London for something like eighteen days. It was quite an adventure, and we got to know each other pretty well," recalls Jonathan. "In fact, we

were like mother and son by the time we got to filming!"

The relationship between the fictional marquis and his mother is not quite so congenial, however. "My mother is, of course, very upset that we have to give up this villa, whereas I'm more accepting of the situation, and I have a lot of reasons to believe that Lord Grantham is my brother. I'm trying to keep everything fun and light when the Crawleys come to visit, and I'm embarrassed by my mother's hostile behavior. The marquis, I think, likes the idea that he might have a brother or another family and feels responsible for his father's legacy."

On seeing the villa that would stand in for the Villa des Colombes, however, Jonathan wasn't so sure he could be as magnanimous as the character he plays: "The villa was amazing. I'm not sure I could ever give that up! The marquis is certainly a very generous man!"

MADAME DE MONTMIRAIL

Nathalie Baye

Madame de Montmirail is distinctly unhappy about having to give up the beautiful Villa des Colombes to a strange English family, and to the great-granddaughter of a former flame of her late husband no less.

When the Crawleys arrive, her welcome is decidedly frosty and not entirely unexpected.

Playing the part of Madame de Montmirail is one of France's best-known actresses, Nathalie Baye. Director Simon Curtis was keen to secure an actress whose talents and experience could match those of Imelda Staunton and Dame Maggie Smith. With over eighty films on her résumé, and a career working with some of cinema's most distinguished directors, Nathalie certainly fit the bill.

Nathalie was very happy to take on the role of the marquis's mother: "*Downton Abbey* is a popular series in France, and when I told my friends about it, they were thrilled! However, I was also a little nervous because I hadn't filmed anything in English for a long time. The cast and crew know one another so well—they are like a family, which is also a little daunting—but they couldn't have been more welcoming or friendly. The experience was wonderful."

Nathalie also found the character she played interesting: "Madame de Montmirail is bitter and very hurt about the situation she finds herself in, but she's going through a range of emotions and is also curious about the Crawleys. Her son is happy to embrace a new family, but she feels very differently. She's from a different generation and does not accept the love story between her husband and Violet."

In fact, Madame de Montmirail is convinced that Violet had a mysterious hold over the late marquis: "She must have blackmailed him," she says in the movie. As a result, the widow is initially determined to challenge her husband's bequest in the courts, despite being told by the family lawyer, Monsieur Gannay, that the legacy is entirely legal and in keeping with the wishes of the late marquis.

"My sense is," says Nathalie, "that Madame de Montmirail never really knew love. I'm not sure she loved her husband —even though she claims she did. And, of course, she came from a period when many marriages were arranged by the family." Jonathan Zaccaï, who plays her son, agrees: "There wasn't much love in the marriage, and she and her son seem a lonely pair."

TRAVELING IN STYLE

To travel to France, the Crawley party must board a cross-channel ferry at Dover, the short voyage to Calais proving most unwelcome for Mr. Carson, who feels decidedly queasy throughout the crossing. To film the scene, the *Downton* cast and crew headed to Leith in Edinburgh, where the Royal Yacht *Britannia*, the former floating palace of Queen Elizabeth, is moored.

"The Royal Yacht *Britannia* was built in around 1952, a little later than our period," relates production designer Donal Woods, "but it worked very well for us and wasn't that different from the ships that were crossing the channel in the late 1920s and 1930s."

On reading the script, supervising location manager Mark "Sparky" Ellis first came up with the idea of using the royal yacht, an ambitious undertaking. In fact, the *Downton Abbey* film crew was the first-ever production unit to shoot on board.

"As soon as Donal and I got on board the yacht, we knew it was right," explains Sparky. "Its teak decks, portholes, and overall size was right for the period. When we were there filming, we did everything on the ship. Costume and makeup were based in the state dining room, which was quite surreal, and we had catering up on the sun decks. . . . Below deck, we had a production office, and we converted two rooms opposite, which were once Prince William and Prince Harry's cabins, into green rooms for Jim Carter and Hugh Bonneville. It was quite a proud moment to have achieved that, to be the first production to shoot on the Royal Yacht *Britannia*, and for a movie like this, you really need to go that extra mile."

The first car-ferry crossing from Dover to Calais, which saw a maximum of fifteen cars winched by crane onto the deck and then lashed in place, was launched in 1928, the year in which *A New Era* is set. The Crawley party, however, has not brought a car with them, as they plan to catch the Blue Train from Calais, a first-class sleeper that, beginning in 1922, whisked the well-heeled and famous to the Mediterranean coast via Paris and Lyon. Its interior was exquisitely crafted in a style that could rival the Savoy Hotel or Simpson's—a mode of transport synonymous with glamour and not an unpleasant way to journey to the Côte d'Azur.

JIM CARTER
MR. CARSON

*"Like Mr. Carson, who suffers
during the cross-channel ferry
crossing to France, I don't have
good sea legs. I can't imagine
Carson has been on anything
bigger than the River Nidd [a
tributary of the River Ouse in
Yorkshire]. The scene was shot
on the Royal Yacht* Britannia,
*and I was pleased it was
moored up to the dock in Leith
in Edinburgh [with movement
added at a later date]."*

4

SILENT TO SOUND MOVIES

As some members of the household head off to the South of France, the cast and crew of the film company, British Lion, descend upon Downton Abbey. They are there to shoot the movie *The Gambler* set in 1875, and the Crawley family home will provide the setting for a country house and gambling club, much to the horror of Robert, who envisages "actresses plastered in makeup and actors just plastered."

However, the large fee that the film's producer and director, Jack Barber, offers will more than pay for the repair of Downton's leaky roof, and before the household knows it, trucks are unloading huge quantities of costumes and lighting and camera equipment, not to mention the star of the film, Myrna Dalgleish, who sweeps inside.

The intention of the filmmakers is to make a silent picture, but production is soon suspended when Jack Barber learns that British Lion intends to shut them down in the face of stiff competition from talking movies, which, as Barber says, "are making too much money to ignore." With the help of Lady Mary, Mr. Molesley, and an immensely self-important and expensive sound technician named Mr. Stubbins, Barber manages to turn the film into a talking picture, despite the precarious logistics and knife-edge financial pressures involved.

THE TALKIES ARRIVE

The year, of course, is 1928, and the first "talking" pictures had just arrived in theaters in the United Kingdom. This new sound cinema would eventually spell the end of silent movies, even though they were hugely popular among filmgoers. *The Jazz Singer* and *The Singing Fool*, both starring US entertainer Al Jolson, were the first projected sound films screened in Britain, though they featured just a few scenes of synchronized dialogue and songs. As Jack Barber explains to Lady Mary, the 1928 US horror film *The Terror* was in fact the first all-talking picture to arrive in Britain, and the long line of filmgoers they observe waiting to see it in nearby Thirsk is a testament to the excitement that surrounded the introduction of talkies.

(Film critics, however, loathed the movie, a murder mystery set in an English country house, calling it "so bad that it is almost suicidal" and causing some to question whether talking pictures had any future at all.)

As Laraine Porter, the historical film consultant on *Downton Abbey: A New Era*, explains, "At that point, even producers in the US were not sure whether talkies were going to catch on or they were just a fad, and the dilemma for filmmakers was whether to bite the bullet and put in the large investment required to fund a talkie or potentially go bust." When it comes to financing the change-over to sound, Jack Barber is in a similar predicament: due to mounting costs, he doesn't have the funds to pay his extras, who decide not to come back to set.

The French silent movie *Napoléon* (1927), written, directed, and produced by Abel Gance, was considered one of the most innovative films in the silent era. Its release, however, coincided with the advent of talking pictures, which proved more of a lure for cinemagoers.

QUOTA QUICKIES

By 1926, the British film industry as a whole had almost gone bankrupt, having experienced something of a slump in the face of the worldwide dominance of Hollywood, and European film companies were similarly finding it difficult to compete. To protect British cinema, the UK government passed the Cinematographic Films Act of 1927, commonly known as the "Quota Act," which required British cinemas to show a certain number of British-made movies. This gave rise to a raft of "quota quickies," the production of hastily produced, low-budget movies, many of which were churned out in as little as two weeks.

While the Quota Act gave UK producers some level of comfort, the arrival of sound caught many in the industry off guard. As a stop gap, silent movies like the fictional film *The Gambler* were retrofitted with dialogue sequences.

But by the end of the decade, the race was on for the British film industry to produce full-length sound features. With filmmakers grappling with the new method of production, the atmosphere was febrile, and of the eight British companies that were set up in January 1929 to make talkies, only one survived into the early 1930s. It was a boom-and-bust environment, and it's no wonder that Jack Barber is nervous about the whole undertaking.

THE SILENT ERA

While talkies had captured the attention of film-going audiences, silent movies were still immensely popular, and the filmmaking process had, as Laraine Porter describes it, reached its apogee during the 1920s. Jack Barber himself refers to the 1927 French silent movie *Napoléon*, written and directed by Abel Gance, which was filmed on location (rather than in a studio) and was seen as a masterpiece of fluid camera motion, full of long close-ups, handheld camera shots, split-screen images, and a gamut of other revolutionary visual effects. And yet the sweeping epic received an indifferent response from US audiences and ultimately proved to be no match for the gimmick of sound pictures.

BLACKMAIL

A notable British filmmaker who emerged in this period was director Alfred Hitchcock, whose first sound film, *Blackmail* (1929), was initially intended as a silent movie, until he was ordered to make it a "part-talkie." Ronald Neame, grandfather of *Downton Abbey*'s producer Gareth Neame, worked on *Blackmail*, and the making of the film inspired the storyline of *Downton Abbey: A New Era*. It was originally intended that only the last act of *Blackmail* would have synchronized dialogue, but Hitchcock balked at the idea. He relished experimenting with dialogue, music, and sound effects in the film, and put them all to use in the production, though the opening sequence of the finished film is without dialogue.

As with Jack Barber's *The Gambler*, some scenes play silent with synchronized sound, while other scenes were completely reworked with sound in mind. This involved having English actress Joan Barry just out of camera range speaking the lines while Czech leading lady Anny Ondra lip-synched them, as her foreign accent was deemed unacceptable. This dubbing process, the first of its kind, is emulated in the *Downton Abbey* movie when Lady Mary provides the voice for Myrna Dalgleish.

Blackmail was heavily marketed as one of Britain's earliest "all-talkie" feature films. A completed silent version was also released in 1929, shortly after the sound version was available in cinemas. It proved a bigger draw and ran longer in cinemas, though this is probably because few UK cinemas at the time were outfitted to project sound film.

The film company depicted in *Downton Abbey* is British Lion, a company that did exist at the time. Founded in 1927, it went on to release many films, including the commercially successful, government-backed *In Which We Serve* in 1942, for which Gareth Neame's grandfather was a cinematographer.

ABOVE Alfred Hitchcock's *Blackmail* (1929) was the first British movie to make use of synchronized sound. Its early methods of filmmaking and sound capture are emulated in *Downton Abbey: A New Era*. **OPPOSITE** Lady Mary provides the voice for Myrna Dalgleish.

JACK BARBER

Hugh Dancy

The success or failure of *The Gambler* weighs heavily on the shoulders of its director and producer, Jack Barber. His arrival, along with that of his stars, extras, and several trucks of equipment, turns Downton Abbey upside down. British Lion has, however, paid for the privilege, and when Lord Grantham attempts to be a little patronizing toward the director, Barber is having none of it.

"What I liked about the character," says Hugh Dancy, the actor who plays Jack Barber, "is that he's an outsider. He's working in this new industry as a creative, but he's also entrepreneurial and a hustler and has to think on his feet a lot of the time. He's unapologetically commercial, the opposite of the Crawleys in that way, and he knows that being at Downton is a mutually beneficial arrangement for all of them. He doesn't really fit into the usual hierarchies. He's perfectly happy to be respectful and polite and knows how to behave, but he doesn't have time for all that window dressing."

As the director of a silent picture, Barber shapes the performances of his actors, even talking to them while they film. To prepare the real actors for their scenes, *Downton Abbey*'s historical film consultant, Laraine Porter, showed some clips from silent movies from the period, which Hugh found particularly revealing: "I'd expected lots of overacting, mascara, that kind of thing, but in fact there was so much artistry, and the acting was underplayed with quite nuanced emotion."

In making the film, Barber faces considerable challenges, and he increasingly relies on Lady Mary not only to provide the voice for his leading lady but also to help him through what is a fraught process. "There's a familiarity between them," explains Hugh, "and she opens up to him. And he knows how to ask questions and guide somebody into revealing themselves a bit." Barber is captivated by Mary, and she has clearly enjoyed working with him. But he's unable to prize a kiss out of her, and Mary, as she later confesses to her sister, has to work hard not to succumb to his obvious charms.

"A good day?"
—LADY MARY

"It's always good if we get through the schedule."
—JACK BARBER

ANNA MARY SCOTT ROBBINS • *Costume Designer*

DOWNTON ABBEY HAS ALWAYS BEEN RENOWNED for its exquisite clothing and mastery of period costume, and over the years, we've seen a vast array of changing fashions, from tight-waisted Edwardian corsets to a much looser silhouette on the ladies, as befits the changing world in which the family lives. Costumes must work perfectly for individual characters as well, symbolizing what they represent. They must also contribute to the storytelling and sit well within the setting and with the other costumes in a shot. It's a complex undertaking overseen by Emmy-nominated costume designer Anna Robbins. "I look at each scene as a composition that needs to be painted beautifully, with all the costumes sitting well together—complementing or contrasting as required by the scene. There is usually a focal point character that I start with and work out from there."

Brought in for the last two seasons of the television series, Anna also worked on the first *Downton* movie, for which she raised the bar even higher with the use of exquisite original pieces and accessories and a meticulous attention to detail. While maintaining those high standards for the big screen, Anna's challenge for the second movie was to create costumes for the very different worlds we see: the silent-film industry, a gambling club of 1875, and the French Riviera. In a more usual setting for *Downton*, Anna did get to design a very special wedding dress for Lucy and to clothe some of the servants in more exotic costumes "I've always wanted to dress the below stairs in proper finery, which I finally managed to do thanks to Julian's clever writing!"

While Anna and her department are familiar with the characters and world of *Downton Abbey*,

The fictional crew for *The Gambler* wheel their elaborate costumes into Downton Abbey.

All three dresses are original pieces. "Edith's russet and silver beaded dress was in perfect condition," recalls Anna. "But we added length, making a slip and some clever hand-beaded sections to better the overall proportion."

there is still a huge amount to do. Her team is made up of a supervisor, design team, workroom, dyeroom, crowd department, and principal truck team, all busy prepping for a new script and running the shoot. For this movie, Anna looked at the script five to six months before shooting and began to get a sense of the story arcs, the characters, and the needs for particular scenes. At the same time, she started sourcing vintage pieces and began putting together initial lineups for the main characters, working with the originals and bespoke designs. For instance, for any given scene there may be perfectly pitched originals for Lady Mary and Lady Edith with the

opportunity to design from scratch for Cora, so she must think about palette, source fabrics, and embellishments for each design.

Hundreds of costumes need to be ready by and during filming, so the logistics are incredibly complex. Each cast member must have a series of fittings. The first fitting can be exploratory, looking at shape, fabric, and colors, often fitting toiles (mock-ups of the design in a plain fabric). The actual fabric is usually used for the second fitting, and then there may be queries at further fittings as the costume is readied for a final check fit. "Everything inches along together," explains Anna, "the sourcing of garments or fabric, the dyeing, the making, and fitting. We work to a shooting schedule, which dictates when each costume is required for filming as per a detailed costume plot for each character. This lineup will itemize what each character is wearing from head to foot in any given scene. Hats, shoes, gloves, and jewelry may need to be sourced or designed and made. As filming starts, this rolling process is still happening, and we are continually establishing costumes on set throughout the shoot."

A costume maker is working on Lucy's wedding dress.

THE FRENCH RIVIERA

Costumes for the French Riviera scenes were both stunning and very different from anything seen before in *Downton Abbey*. "We wanted to create a relaxed feel," explains Anna Robbins. "Back in the UK, everything is set against dark wood, and the fabrics are darker and more opulent. In France, there's this saturated sunlight and Mediterranean decor, and everything's paler, which lends itself more to Neapolitan sorbet-like colors. And for the first time, we see the gents in creamy pale linen."

"We were able to dress Lady Edith in quite daring clothes, including an original matching printed silk pajama set, which was all the rage on the French Riviera at that time," says Anna. "She also wore beautiful palazzo pants—and it's a rare sight in *Downton Abbey* to see the ladies in trousers—along with an original art deco printed jacket."

ANNA ROBBINS
COSTUME DESIGNER

"When traveling on the ferry and on the boat in the French Riviera, we see Lord Grantham looking quintessentially British and in separates for the first time. On the ferry, he wears a Grenadier Guards boating jacket with regimental brass buttons, Grenadier Guards regimental tie, and gray flannel trousers. On the boat, he dons a similar Royal Yacht Squadron look, complete with cap and squadron tie pin."

ANNA ROBBINS
COSTUME DESIGNER

"Lucy and Edith are in original vintage dresses, which are very on point in terms of 1920s sportswear. Tom wears an original Airtex shirt, and Bertie is in an original knit. The men are in high-waisted trousers, and we even see Tom's belt—a first for Downton, as the men are always in suits or waistcoats— and with rolled-up sleeves, everything feels more relaxed."

ANNA ROBBINS
COSTUME DESIGNER

"Mary's dress came from Paris and was in perfect condition. It is covered in starbursts of gold sequins on black, which look like lots of spotlights. I usually use sequins sparingly and tend to favor beadwork, but this dress was so stunning in terms of impact, and the asymmetric hem was very on trend. Mary wears it to dinner when Myrna is first introduced to the family, so I wanted to up the Hollywood glamour stakes for them both."

ANNE "NOSH" OLDHAM • *Hair & Makeup Designer*

"I'VE ALWAYS TRIED REALLY HARD WITH Downton to give it the feel of a working house. This is home for many of the characters, so I don't want it to look like a fashion piece," comments award-winning hair and makeup designer Anne "Nosh" Oldham. Her work, nonetheless, is a key component of *Downton*'s exquisite look, having initially established the key silhouettes and appearances of all the main characters for the first two seasons and then finessing them further still for the first movie.

This time around, Nosh's aim was to refresh all the characters and bring them slightly forward in period. She had a highly skilled team around her including fantastic wigmakers and makeup artists who gave everything beautiful attention to detail.

Nosh Oldham applies makeup to Jim Carter (Mr Carson).

ANNE "NOSH"
OLDHAM
HAIR & MAKEUP DESIGNER
*"A challenge for hair and
makeup was to create looks
that would work both in color
and on the black-and-white
screen. We put some eye makeup on Guy to make him a little
more like Rudolph Valentino,
one of the biggest silent-screen
stars; added some sideburns;
and paled him down a bit.
We made Myrna a little paler
with darker lipstick, as you
need greater depth of tone with
black-and-white images."*

For the silent-movie stars and crew who descend on Downton Abbey, Nosh and her team were able to create looks that were very different from those seen before among members of the Crawley household. Central to this was the character of Myrna Dalgleish, played by Laura Haddock, who Nosh describes as something of a "visual shock" to everyone at Downton: "She's a beautiful woman, just as Lady Mary is, but they're polar opposites. Myrna is an outsider, and we wanted to create a look where she doesn't really fit into any setting. With her platinum blonde hair and lots of makeup, she's a real Jean Harlow (top and bottom left) figure, the original blonde bombshell film star of the period. We also drew on the appearance of a number of other movie idols of the era, with Hollywood star Constance Bennett (bottom right) becoming the main inspiration for Myrna's look."

ABOVE Jack Barber has longer, more bohemian-style hair that was modeled on the Bloomsbury set artist Duncan Grant. **BELOW** Another new character who comes to Downton and really does seem like he's from another planet is the sound technician, Mr. Stubbins, played by Alex Macqueen. "I was told that if there's any actor who will take on a look and really run with it, it's Alex," recalls Nosh. "I looked at all sorts of references and found an image of a German-officer type with this miniscule Poirot-like moustache. I fell in love with it, suggested it to the producers, assuming that I would not be allowed to go for it, but they said yes! And it's my winning look, I think, of the whole film!"

ANNE "NOSH"
OLDHAM

HAIR & MAKEUP DESIGNER

"We had the best fun dressing
up the servants. They
have ringlets, feathers, and
outrageous hairdos."

ANNE "NOSH" OLDHAM

HAIR & MAKEUP DESIGNER

"Daisy's hair is quite different for this movie. As Sophie's hair is longer now, Daisy has two little plaited buns, which we thought looked sweet. Anna's hair is similar to the last film. She has a period bob with a bit of marcel waving. It's a nod to the fashions going on upstairs."

ANNE "NOSH"
OLDHAM
HAIR & MAKEUP DESIGNER

*"Lady Mary has a bob, but
it's longer now, with a side
parting and no fringe or the
really chiseled cut she had in
the first movie."*

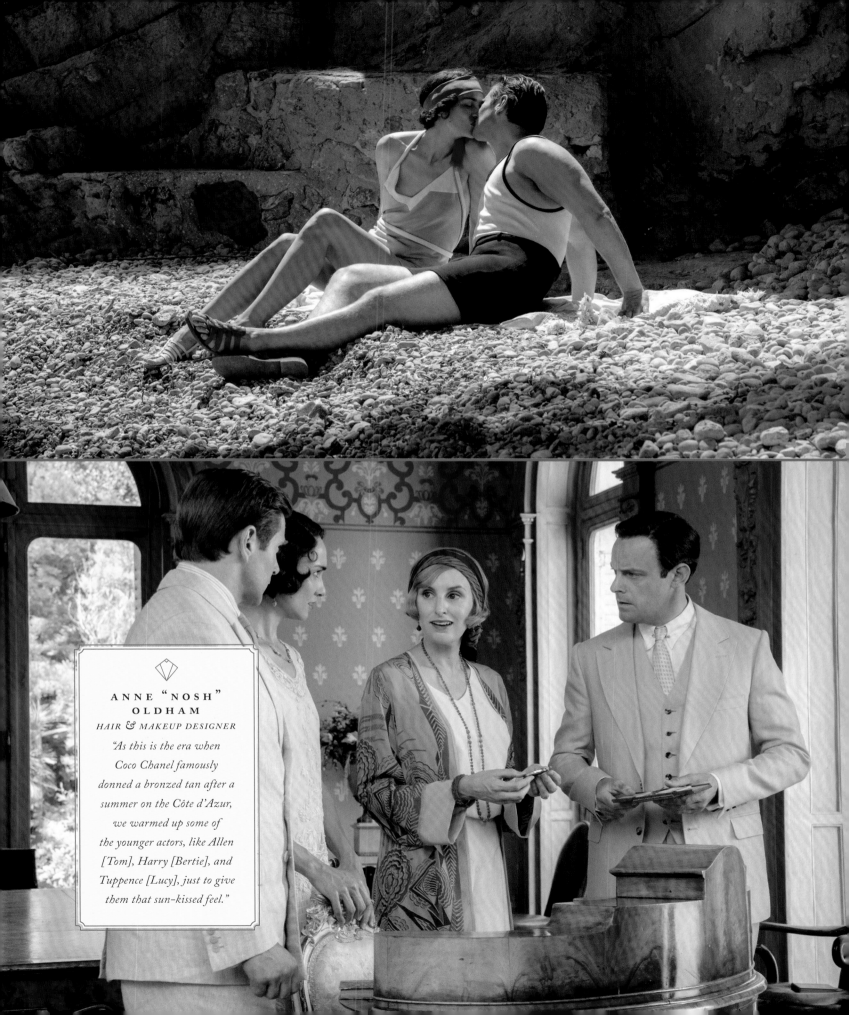

MR. STUBBINS

Alex Macqueen

In order to turn *The Gambler* into a talking movie, the director Jack Barber must enlist the services of a sound technician, who would record and synthesize the all-important sound for the movie.

The plan was to record the sound and speech for the scenes that had already been shot, requiring Guy Dexter and Lady Mary (standing in for Myrna Dalgleish) to speak into a stand-alone microphone and to ensure their words matched the images playing on a projector screen. For new scenes, they would record the sound as they filmed, with extra lines supplied by Mr. Molesley.

Mr. Stubbins is the sound technician, and we sense from the outset that he is all too aware of his own importance and status. With his peculiar little moustache and mustard-colored suit, Mr. Stubbins immediately sets about lording it over the film set: "If he could," says Alex Macqueen, who plays Stubbins, "he would have said 'action' and 'cut'—and directed the whole thing." As was the experience of filmmakers of the time, the arrival of Mr. Stubbins serves to disrupt not only a process that has been honed over thirty years but also the close working relationships that had often developed among the director, cameraman, and key actors. It is almost as if an alien has arrived from a very different world.

Sound technology was indeed viewed as more of a science than an art, and Stubbins has no interest in the artistic merit of the production, advising Guy Dexter to "time your speech to match the film. No, no, no, don't lean in and try not to move your head, all right. Ring the bell for silence." To Stubbins, explains Alex, "the director is of zero importance, the stars are a bit of a nuisance, and ultimately the whole project is about the sound.

"It was a brand-new technology at the time," continues Alex. "It was in its infancy, so he had every right to think he was at the very cutting edge of technology and change, but he certainly takes it to a more extreme degree." As awful as he is, however, Mr. Stubbins and other sound technicians did represent the future of filmmaking, and directors like Jack Barber would learn to harness the power of sound to their advantage. Technology would eventually adapt as well, so actors could move around freely and convey plenty of emotion whenever a scene demanded it.

SIMON CURTIS • *Director*

ANY DIRECTOR OF *DOWNTON ABBEY* MUST oversee a large ensemble cast made up of some of the very best of British acting talent. It's a challenge that Simon Curtis was more than capable of taking on, despite not having worked on the series before. Simon knew the majority of the cast and many of the crew, and had worked with Penelope Wilton, Dame Maggie Smith, Hugh Bonneville, and Imelda Staunton across a large body of theater, television, and film productions. He also happens to be married to Elizabeth McGovern, who plays Cora, so he knows something of the behind-the-scenes family that has developed over the years.

Nonetheless, directing such a large body of exceptional actors still took some getting used to: "There might be a one-line scene and half of British equity would turn up," jokes Simon. "For something like the big scene in Violet's bedroom, you'd have two of the greatest British actresses sitting on a sofa for a whole day, almost as if they were extras. I always treat everyone in the cast like they are leading actors. That was quite exhausting across thirteen weeks of filming with such a large cast, but I enjoyed it because I have such admiration for the cast and like them so much."

Downton Abbey also features a large number of interweaving storylines and scenes, and one of the most challenging for Simon was the film-within-the-film dining room scene in which the servants play extras. "It was shot over three days, required forty-eight camera angles, and included actors in gigantic costumes, the Crawley family looking on, the fake movie crew, and the real crew. It also included two couples committing to each other, rather like Act V of a Shakespeare play, and to get around all of this, we broke the scene down into six small scenes, filming Molesley's proposal separately."

A key player working alongside Simon was cinematographer Andrew Dunn. "A veteran of sixty feature films, including Julian Fellowes's Oscar-winning *Gosford Park*, Andrew was my principal collaborator throughout the whole shoot," says Simon. His way of working included using an anamorphic lens on a digital camera, which made the wide-screen effects of shooting in 35mm possible but also required more lights and focus pulling. Producer Liz Trubridge described the use of the lens as adding "real beauty to the filming—everything looks like it's hanging in a gallery." Simon and Andrew also made use of drones and cranes for sweeping aerial shots and of other specialized equipment that added to the scope of the movie.

ABOVE Simon Curtis is very much an actor's director. He's a great admirer of their skill and had previously worked with many of the cast members of *Downton Abbey*. **OPPOSITE** Simon discusses a scene with Sophie McShera (Daisy) on the set of the Downton kitchen.

Alongside directing complex scenes with a large cast, Simon and the production crew had to contend with the logistics of shooting during the Covid pandemic, which required administering over fourteen thousand Covid tests across the thirteen weeks of filming. Despite the potential pitfalls and the obstacles thrown their way, Simon and his team managed to get through the shooting schedule and were delighted to film in France, where they could make full use of the extraordinary setting.

The role of director is never an easy task, however, and Simon did joke that there was something cathartic in giving notes to actor Hugh Dancy about how to play the part of a frustrated director trying to pull everything together—"it echoes how I feel at times." Despite the challenge, Simon was a very natural fit on set, collaborative with the production crew and an actor's director. As producer Liz Trubridge says, "If the cast are happy—and they were delighted with Simon—we are too."

THE MAKING OF EARLY SOUND MOVIES

As the filming of a silent and then early sound movie formed an integral part of *A New Era*, the production team brought in advisers to help them with various aspects of the storyline and the techniques of early filmmaking. Laraine Porter, associate professor and senior lecturer in cinema history at Leicester's De Montfort University and a specialist in silent and early sound movies, was a key consultant who advised the team during the production of the film.

An essential part of Laraine's role was to advise on the stark differences between the film set of a silent picture and that of an early sound movie, and how that might be portrayed on screen. "Compared to the sets of movies today," explains Laraine, "silent-movie sets were very noisy places. In filming a scene, the director could give verbal instructions to performers, telling them perhaps how their character is feeling and when to say their line." Director Jack Barber does exactly this with actress Myrna Dalgleish: "Walk downstairs and find him with your eyes. You halt and walk on but he's waiting for you. Tell her she looks beautiful. You're delighted to hear it but you cannot admit it. You look into his eyes. . . ." By being so descriptive, he provides a less-confident actress like Myrna plenty of support and direction. There is also a pianist tinkling away, and other sets might have had a string quartet playing music during filming to help the actors emote or get them in the right mood for a scene.

"The sound set, however, was very different," Laraine continues. "The set had to be silent, with no talking, and the camera could no longer move around. All that camaraderie and the direction that the director can give to his stars—getting so close that he can almost whisper in their ears—suddenly goes."

When the first talking movies came on the scene, filmmakers had two ways of recording and synchronizing sound. It could be recorded directly onto a film track, usually the same film strip onto which the moving picture had been recorded, or onto separate

discs or phonograph records that were played on a turn-table and could record and play back sound in sync with a movie. While sound on film would become the more commonly used process, some early talkies, such as *The Jazz Singer* and *The Terror*, utilized the sound-on-disc system, or Vitaphone as it was coined by Warner Brothers, and it is the technology used in the making of *The Gambler* in *Downton Abbey: A New Era*.

To re-create this type of sound capture, the *Downton* production crew were keen to source authentic pieces of

The cameraman for *The Gambler* sits in a large insulated box, which was specially built for the movie.

equipment from the period, which, due to their rarity, required the help of collectors of early film props who had salvaged and faithfully restored specialist items. One such contraption was a sound-on-disc machine, which had been rescued from a skip and restored by a collector and is now the only one in the country. In the movie, we can even see it cutting the recording discs, which was a first for Laraine, and it "worked beautifully."

In filming a scene for an early sound movie, actors were also required to remain largely motionless when speaking because their microphones had limited range and were stationary, either hidden behind an object on set or hanging on a cable at a specific position just above camera range. This is why Mr. Stubbins, who is anxious to have the microphones pick up every word of dialogue, asks the actors not to move their heads during a scene. (The 1952 Hollywood movie *Singin' in the Rain*, which depicts a 1927 film, famously shows exactly what actors and directors were up against when filming an early talkie using fixed microphones.) It took a short while for filmmakers to hit upon the idea of placing the mike on a boom, or long stick just out of view of the camera, which could then follow the action.

As a result, the early sound movies had a stiff feel, with actors forced to reduce their range of movement, not to mention deliver dialogue for the first time. Clara Bow, one of the most popular Hollywood stars of the silent screen, notably complained at the time: "I hate talkies . . . they're stiff and limiting. You lose a lot of your cuteness, because there's no chance for action, and action is the most important thing to me." Many filmmakers, such as Hollywood director King Vidor, felt they had developed a unique kind of art form in silent pictures, only to be constrained by the need to introduce sound: "We were busting forth with a fresh channel of expression in each new movie. . . . Then, bang, we were hit with this sound thing, and the technicians began to dominate the scene. 'You can't do that, you can't move there, you can't speak with your head down.'"

Early microphones could also pick up sound made near them on set, including the whir of a camera. For that reason, the camera and its operator had to be encased in a large padded box—as we see in the movie—making them far less mobile than those used for silent movies and further adding to the static nature of early sound films. Much quieter cameras were soon developed, so the insulated boxes were in use for only two or three years. For that reason, none have survived the passage of time, and a box needed to be specially built, following historical references, for *A New Era*. "The day I arrived at Ealing Studios and saw the box that had been constructed for the sound camera," recalls Laraine, "I actually felt really emotional. This amazing object hadn't been seen since 1929 or 1930, and they had crafted it so perfectly."

When recording sound for *The Gambler*, Mr. Stubbins, the sound technician, sits at a sound monitor box, using headphones to listen and adjust the sound. While on a studio set, the crew would have had a much larger sound setup, with a monitoring booth connected to a separate recording machine, all designed to amplify the sound. On a location shoot like *Downton Abbey*, a more rudimentary sound kit would have been used. In the gambling club scene, we see a sound effects man sweeping chips off the table in sync with the French croupier who is working the roulette table. Unlike modern movies, where Foley artists can add sound effects and enhance the audio quality after filming, early sound movies recorded everything while shooting on set, so any sound effect would be created as the camera rolled.

Albert, the junior footman, operates a clapperboard, which helps filmmakers synchronize the picture and sound and shows which scene is being filmed. Early sound movies improvised with various types of contraptions, such as long, thin "clappersticks."

5

STARS OF THE
SILVER SCREEN

There are members of the Downton Abbey household who are thrilled that a film production company is moving in. Chief among them is Mr. Molesley, who clearly enjoys a trip to the pictures. Anna and Daisy are similarly excited and are seen poring over movie magazines that are filled with images of their favorite screen idols, including Guy Dexter and Myrna Dalgleish.

Jack Barber, the film's director, and Lady Mary decide to head to the Rialto cinema in nearby Thirsk to see Myrna Dalgleish's latest movie. Driving along the high street, they pass a cinema that has a long queue and a "Sold Out" board outside, and Barber explains that the line is for the evidently more popular talking picture *The Terror*. They nonetheless press on to the Rialto, take their seat in the almost-empty auditorium, and watch the movie, which is accompanied by a small orchestra, after which they stand for the national anthem.

It would have been entirely appropriate at the time for a town like Thirsk to have on its high street at least two cinemas, or "picture palaces" as they were known. Filmgoers relished the escapism movies provided, a world away from the realities of everyday life, with Mr. Molesley describing Hollywood as "the ultimate dream factory, and I need dreams as much as the next man." Silent movies were immensely popular, but the advent of sound would further boost ticket sales, as Lady Mary and Jack Barber's experience in Thirsk shows.

Such was the appeal of going to the cinema that by 1929, half of the adult population of Britain was going to the cinema at least once a week, a trend also reflected across Europe and in the United States. By now, Hollywood was producing some five hundred films each year, and the introduction of audio saw a huge leap in cinema going, rising from 60 million Americans going on a weekly basis in 1927 to 110 million by 1929. In the United Kingdom, virtually every town had a permanent picture house by 1914, with some three thousand cinemas across the country in 1926, rising to forty-five hundred by 1929. As *Downton's* historical film consultant Laraine Porter describes, "By the late 1920s, a city like Leicester had twenty cinemas, and across the country, picture palaces were popping up not only in urban centers but also in the rapidly expanding suburbs, at the end of tram lines, in workplaces, and as part of every major housing development of the period."

Where once the music hall was the biggest form of entertainment in the United Kingdom, this role was now filled by the cinema, and by 1929, more people went to the pictures than football matches. The appeal was not just with the movies and the thrilling beginning of sound but also in the cinemas themselves, many of which had opulent, richly decorated interiors and flamboyant art deco exteriors, exhibiting, as Laraine puts it, "the most creative vernacular architecture of their time." Regional theater chains also began to appear, along with the construction of vast new picture palaces in major cities. Among the most famous was the now-demolished Regent in Brighton, which opened in 1921 and was one of Britain's first "super-cinemas," with over two thousand seats and a restaurant, café, tearoom, and dance hall above the auditorium. Other large cinemas were constructed around the country, with one of the biggest, Glasgow's Green Playhouse, opening in 1927 with 4,254 seats. As women made up the biggest sector in the audience, some picture palaces had creches and offered hand creams and lotions, all designed to entice film lovers.

Where silent movies were played—and it took a few years for picture palaces to adapt to sound movies—they were accompanied by a pianist, string quartet, or, as in the case of Thirsk, a small orchestra. Dialogue would appear on intertitles or dialogue cards, which were sometimes read out by members of the audience for those who couldn't read. And as we see in *A New Era*, the national anthem was generally played at the end of a film program. Cinemas had a range of ticket prices, from around four or five pence for the standard seats, rising to seven pence halfpenny for the more comfortable, plush seats. The picture palaces of the late 1920s were not only comfortable and exciting but also affordable places where Anna, Daisy, and Mr. Molesley could escape to a very different world.

The Electric Palace in Harwich, Essex provided the exterior and interior for the Rialto cinema in Thirsk. Beautifully restored and dating back to 1911, it is one of the oldest purpose-built cinemas to survive in the United Kingdom.

LARAINE PORTER
HISTORICAL FILM ADVISER

"To ensure his movie is a commercial success, Jack Barber must turn it into a talking picture. To begin filming a scene, he uses the words 'ring the bell, roll the camera, and action'—the bell signaling the start of sound recording, which required total silence on set. In contrast, silent movie sets were much noisier, and the director could talk to the actors as the camera rolled."

GUY DEXTER

Dominic West

Guy Dexter, played by Dominic West, is the matinee idol who arrives at Downton Abbey. Like his costar, Myrna Dalgleish, his film-star good looks and magnetic presence— "like a wild animal ready to spring," as Daisy puts it—exude the kind of glamour that can only come from Hollywood.

Despite his California sheen, Guy has—to Lady Mary's surprise—an English accent. We learn that he headed off to the United States ten years earlier and is now part of the so-called Hollywood Raj, a group of British actors who carved out careers in the US film industry. Guy Dexter is clearly very much part of the film-star set, casually mentioning his acquaintance with one of the biggest silent-movie stars of the era, Charlie Chaplin.

The character of Guy Dexter is typical of the type of silent-movie actor of the period, and Julian Fellowes in fact had the English-born actor Ronald Colman in mind when he created Dexter. His Hollywood swagger, however, belies his lack of confidence in his acting abilities. He is not a trained actor and originally worked in a menswear shop, where he was spotted posing for a trade journal. So, like Myrna, he is deeply worried about whether he can make it in the talkies: "They won't want us.

They'll hire real actors from the theatre, and we'll be finished."

Guy finds himself confiding in Downton's butler, Thomas Barrow (played by Robert James-Collier), who has clearly caught his eye. The two men develop something of a connection, resulting in Guy suggesting to Thomas that he move to Los Angeles with him where he can work as his dresser. Thomas, who can't quite believe his luck, readily accepts, knowing that he has been presented with a once-in-a-lifetime opportunity to find happiness with another man. It's a neat solution for Guy Dexter as well. As a romantic lead, he would have needed to keep his homosexuality out of the public eye, but a private arrangement such as this would have attracted little comment in Hollywood. It's also apparent that Guy has the acting ability and charisma to do well in the talkies, and with Thomas by his side, the two are destined for an exciting future.

MOVIE STAR FASHION

The movie stars and film crew who descend on Downton Abbey inhabit a very different world from the Crawley household, and their appearance should reflect that. The costume, hair, and makeup departments were delighted to meet that challenge, and much of their inspiration came from real silent-movie stars of the period.

The fictional screen star Myrna Dalgleish, played by Laura Haddock, oozes movie glamour, and her appearance is strikingly different from anything ever seen at Downton Abbey. "We wanted her to have the feel of a quintessential Hollywood star," explains costume designer Anna Robbins. "Her platinum blonde hair worked beautifully with icier cool tones, so we used cool peaches and pinks, icy turquoises and blues, and a palette that meant she popped in every setting and room of Downton Abbey.

"We also got to play with amazing textures and textiles with Myrna—with lots of big sleeves, marabou feathers, and long trains, all of which provide drama and complement the way she acts and holds herself."

In re-creating the Hollywood look, Anna was also mindful that *Downton Abbey* has reached the late 1920s, when certain elements

"We wanted her to have the feel of a quintessential Hollywood star."

of style associated with the 1930s start to emerge. We see those modern touches on Guy Dexter, played by Dominic West, who in one scene wears a double-breasted evening jacket, a look that became increasingly fashionable in the 1930s. "He is a British actor but living in Hollywood," says Anna, "so we were able to bring in a few American influences for what he wears. For example, his ties are slightly different from their British equivalent, as are the cut of his jackets and the various cloths his suits are made from, and they all come together to create the look of a Hollywood leading man.

The director, Jack Barber, played by Hugh Dancy, also represents a world rarely seen at Downton Abbey, that of the working professional. He wears more of a deconstructed suit, which allows him to move around easily, with different ties, and he'll roll up his shirtsleeves if he's on a hot film set."

"Having spent ten years standing behind posh people who don't know how to feed themselves, I finally got to sit down during a dining room scene. It was small payback for those years spent dodging around cameras to pour my soft drink [standing in for red wine] on cue."

JIM CARTER
MR. CARSON

ANNA ROBBINS
COSTUME DESIGNER

"Dressing the downstairs servants in 1875 finery elevated them to a different space, and they looked so glorious! The Gambler *is set in the 1870s, but we purposely had elements of the 1920s seeping in, so the 1870s design and silhouettes were mixed with 1928 makeup, jewelery, and fabric from the period. To research this, we looked at various period dramas, such as the theater production of* The Importance of Being Earnest, *which was set in 1875 but staged in the late 1920s, as well as the Civil War epic* Gone with the Wind, *made in 1939, to see how the period in which something is made also permeates the setting and style of a production."*

MYRNA DALGLEISH

Laura Haddock

Film star Myrna Dalgleish sweeps into Downton Abbey, looking every inch a goddess of the silver screen. Draped in icy-blue chiffon, her hair a dazzling peroxide blonde, she seems to glow from every pore. Her manners and conversation, however, are not quite as polished, which comes as something of a shock to the Crawley household.

The casting of Myrna was somewhat of a challenge for the *Downton Abbey* producers, and Laura Haddock played the role to perfection. "For Myrna, we were looking for very specific things," explains producer Liz Trubridge. "She's very glamorous, but she's not a one-dimensional character, and she's terrified about the talkies arriving. We needed someone who could deliver that nuanced performance; otherwise, she would just be seen as unbearable. And I think Laura had enormous fun playing her."

When Myrna first meets the Crawleys, she's rude to the servants and uncouth when chatting with the family at dinner, telling Edith that her rise to fame is not as romantic as it might seem—"not when you know that every man in the room just wants to give you one." Aware that her fame rests purely on her looks, Myrna's worst fears are confirmed when the decision is made to turn the movie into a talking picture, and it's clear she lacks the refined accent necessary to play a titled

lady. When Lady Mary steps in to provide her voice, Myrna struggles with the miming and, humiliated, storms off set, later shouting, "I knew I was finished the moment I saw *The Jazz Singer*! It's been a sword hanging over me."

With all of Myrna's paranoia pouring out, Anna and Daisy attempt to calm her down, though not before Daisy admonishes her for her earlier rudeness, reminding her that as the daughter of a market trader her background is not unlike her own. Lady Grantham eventually suggests Myrna try an American accent, which to everyone's astonishment she pulls off remarkably well. As a result, just before she leaves Downton Abbey, she thanks Anna and Daisy for "licking her into shape" and gives junior footman Albert, who has been entirely starstruck since Myrna's arrival, a peck on the cheek. Then she goes on her way, hopeful that she can continue to shimmer on the screen in Hollywood.

CHARLIE WATSON
ALBERT

When Myrna Dalgleish first arrives at Downton, Albert instantly develops a schoolboy crush on her. "Laura Haddock, who plays Myrna, was in reality so beautiful that I felt a little like that on set—no acting needed! After each take when Myrna kisses Albert, I had a massive lipstick mark on my cheek."

SCREEN IDOLS

Movie stars Myrna Dalgleish and Guy Dexter cause something of a stir when they arrive at Downton Abbey. Although they radiate Hollywood glamour, we learn they are both from ordinary backgrounds—Myrna's family were market traders and Guy once worked in a men's clothing store. But they are blessed with good looks, which has brought them fame and riches.

They represent the type of silent-film stars who were worshipped by filmgoers in the 1920s, their names splashed on film posters as a way to draw in the crowds.

Such was the interest in screen idols of the period that magazines, photos, and even cigarette cards featured images of some of the best-loved movie stars and became cherished possessions of movie lovers. Fan magazines, in particular, gave audiences a way to indulge in the magic of the movies and were capitalized on by the film industry looking to promote their stars and upcoming films. Daisy and Anna each have film magazines that feature glossy images of *The Gambler* stars, Guy looking like the swashbuckling hero and Myrna looking impossibly sensational on the cover of *Picturegoer* with the strapline, "Myrna Dalgleish—A beauty on screen."

As women made up a large part of the

film-going audience, fan magazines were increasingly targeted at females during the 1920s and were priced to make them affordable for all. Inside pages might include

Myrna Dalgleish shimmers on the cover of *Picturegoer*, one of the most popular movie fan magazines of the 1920s.

interviews with stars, stories on newly released films, behind-the-scenes movie gossip, actor-endorsed advertising, advice columns, and a variety of articles on fashion, dressmaking, and cosmetics, along with notices about upcoming films. *Picturegoer* was the most popular British fan magazine of the period, aimed at women who "enjoyed cinema-going as part of a modern and aspirational lifestyle." Its glamorous portraits of film stars proved popular with readers, as did its insights into the off-screen home lives of many of the stars.

Hollywood, of course, produced some of the biggest stars of the period. Among them were Dorothy Gish, who was brought to England in the mid-1920s to boost film production; Clara Bow, the ultimate "it girl"; Douglas Fairbanks, who was known for his swashbuckling roles; and British-born Charlie Chaplin, whose "Tramp" figure and comedic turns had earned him worldwide fame. The most popular British stars in the 1920s were the Welsh actor and composer Ivor Novello, whose many talents and good looks earned him much acclaim, and Betty Balfour, who delighted audiences in the United Kingdom and Europe with her expressive comedic style and charm, though her career would not be matched during the talking-picture era.

TALKIE TERROR

For silent-movie actors, the advent of sound brought with it a certain amount of anxiety, or "talkie terror" as it was

CLOCKWISE FROM TOP LEFT Dorothy Gish, Clara Bow, Douglas Fairbanks, Charlie Chaplin, Ivor Novello, and Betty Balfour were some of the biggest stars in the 1920s, adored by cinema-going audiences in the United Kingdom, United States, and across Europe.

dubbed by some gossip magazines. Alongside action and expression, actors now had to learn and deliver dialogue, and clarity of voice was the important factor for directors embracing the new technology. This proved problematic for actors with heavy foreign or regional accents, or for stars like our fictional Myrna or Guy, who had little or no formal acting training. Myrna's Cockney accent is entirely wrong for her character of Lady Anne Erskine, necessitating Lady Mary to step in and lend her aristocratic tone to the film. "Myrna literally has her voice taken away from her," explains historical film consultant Laraine Porter, "and sees her career vanishing. She would have been terrified."

While some actors failed to flourish in the sound era—perhaps because their careers were nearing an end anyway—there were plenty who successfully made the transition. Even Clara Bow retained her stardom, despite her strong Brooklyn accent and hatred for the new medium, saying, "I can't buck progress. I have to do the best I can." Theater-trained actors had the best advantage, of course, as they were used to learning lines and delivering them in a way that would be audible to audiences.

The character of Guy Dexter was inspired by British actor Ronald Colman, who successfully made the transition from silent to talking movies, helped by his image as an archetypal English gentleman and by his almost lyrical, mellifluous speaking voice that so enchanted Hollywood producer Samuel Goldwyn that he put Colman under contract for almost the rest of his life. However, his leading lady, the Hungarian actress Vilma Bánky, fared less well in the talkies. In the 1920s, she and Colman were one of the biggest romantic couples on screen, and she was a major silent-film star in her own right in Europe and the United States. When the talkies came, she made a handful of pictures and charmed Hollywood with her attempts to pronounce the English language—on arrival in Los Angeles, she is quoted as saying, "I spik no Engleesh, but, oh, these beautiful air of Angelees!"—but she never felt comfortable in the medium and made her last film, *The Rebel*, in 1932.

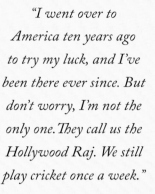

"I went over to America ten years ago to try my luck, and I've been there ever since. But don't worry, I'm not the only one. They call us the Hollywood Raj. We still play cricket once a week."

—GUY DEXTER

HOLLYWOOD RAJ

Like Guy Dexter, Ronald Colman moved to Los Angeles and established himself as one of the richest and most successful of the Hollywood Raj, a group of British actors who had colonized parts of Hollywood in the 1920s and 1930s, their accents and theater training earning them movie roles and a place in the Californian sun. London-born Charlie Chaplin, whom Guy mentions in the movie, was an early inhabitant of Tinseltown and was, by 1928, a global figure and major player in the Hollywood film industry. Members of the Hollywood Raj, who were known for living an expat life of cricket and Sunday-afternoon teas, included leading men Herbert Marshall and Clive Brook and a later generation led by Cary Grant and David Niven, whose officer-and-gentleman acting style recalled Ronald Colman.

Silent-film star Vilma Bánky fared less well in the talkies than her costar Ronald Colman, who continued to dazzle Hollywood.

"I'm not an actress."
—LADY MARY

"Is Myrna an actress?
Are you keen to see
her Hedda Gabler?"
—JACK BARBER

THOMAS BARROW
Robert James-Collier

The arrival of a film crew and its glamorous stars is set to have a dramatic effect on the life of Downton Abbey's butler, Thomas Barrow. Having worked his way up from hall boy to butler, he tells Guy Dexter, "There's not much I couldn't tell you about how to run a house."

His years at Downton Abbey, however, have not been easy: once sharp-tongued and sometimes unkind to those around him, he has nonetheless led a difficult life, forced to conceal his homosexuality, which has in turn exposed his more sensitive side.

That struggle has driven Thomas, played by Robert James-Collier, to the very brink of despair, attempting even to take his own life until his longtime support, Miss Baxter, raised the alarm. Past romantic relationships have never gone well for Thomas, though there was a glimmer of hope when he met royal valet Mr. Ellis in the last movie. Barrow subsequently learns, however, that Mr. Ellis has married, choosing the path that, as Mrs. Hughes describes, most people in his position do to "hide behind appearances that will allow them to avoid persecution and rejection."

Out of everyone at Downton Abbey, Thomas faces the most obstacles in finding a way of life that will make him happy. This was a very difficult period to be a homosexual, deemed in the late 1920s (and up to 1967) an illegal offense subject to imprisonment or hard labor, not to mention harassment and ostracism from society at large. As a result, Thomas is destined to live a lonely life until he has the good fortune to meet handsome movie star Guy Dexter, who operates in very different circles from that of a butler living in Yorkshire and, from their first meeting, is clearly attracted to Mr. Barrow.

Guy confides in Thomas, laying bare his worries about his future career in talking pictures, while Thomas finds himself in the rather strange position of reassuring the film star. The pair bond quickly, and Guy suggests that Thomas move with him to Hollywood as his dresser. Thomas, almost in disbelief, is nonetheless keen to accept: "It's the nearest I've come to the offer of an honest way of life," he says to Lady Mary, as he hands in his notice. Thomas has, in his own way, been swept off his feet. Because of Guy's offer, he can at last explore who he really is and have a chance at living happily ever after.

The cast play frisbee between takes, though they still need to be mindful that they're in costume.

6

THE LIFE OF
VIOLET GRANTHAM

The indisputable matriarch of the Crawley family, Violet, the Dowager Countess, remains a formidable presence at Downton Abbey. After a long life, her time is now running out, and she has moved back to Downton with her maid, Denker. She is ailing physically and unable to attend Tom and Lucy's wedding, but her mind is as sharp as ever. She is still very much Violet.

The Dowager Countess has never been afraid to share her opinions, and as "Granny" to Mary, Edith, and Sybil and now a great-grandmother, she sees it as her duty to protect her family from their own misjudgments. Born in 1842, she had an aristocratic upbringing, and while she didn't make the rules of the society into which she was born, she certainly learned them and lived them, and frequently expresses her horror over the steady erosion of those rules. "So another brick is pulled from the wall," she exclaimed in the series when she first saw Robert in black tie rather than the usual tails required for dinner. Of the need for servants she said, "An aristocrat with no servants is as much use to the county as a glass hammer," and when cousin Isobel reminded her that "servants are human beings too," Violet retorted, "Yes. But preferably only on their days off."

While Violet may delight in voicing a certain snobbery, hankering after a past in which everyone seemed to know their place, she doesn't let that snobbery "dictate her actions or choices," as her creator Julian Fellowes puts it. When it comes to the upkeep of the Downton estate, Violet can be decidedly pragmatic, perhaps because her baronet father was impoverished by the time she married Patrick Crawley, the sixth Earl of Grantham. It's for that reason that she chooses to pass on her newly acquired French villa to granddaughter Sybbie, so she can ensure Sybbie has, like her cousins, the security of an inheritance. And unlike her son, Robert, Violet can instantly see the benefits of allowing a film crew into the house, answering Mary when she queries whether she thinks the idea common, "Nothing is too common if it will help to keep Downton afloat."

Violet is also more worldly than she might let on, as tantalizing glimpses into the exploits of her younger years suggest. More is revealed in the movie when the Crawley family learn of a mysterious French nobleman, the Marquis de Montmirail, who has bequeathed to Violet his villa in the South of France. It emerges that Violet had stayed at the marquis's villa not long after she married, all of which raises a few questions among the family, not least the delicate matter as to who might have fathered Robert, born the following year. Violet explains to the family that on her return, the marquis had written to inform her that he had transferred the villa to her name. But she had never thought he was serious nor did she see him again, knowing that she might succumb to the handsome Frenchman if she did.

However, it would seem Violet hadn't quite got over her predilection for foreign noblemen, as just a few years later, in 1874, she almost got herself into "terrible trouble" with a Russian nobleman, Prince Igor Kuragin, until she was sent back to her husband. As Violet herself admits to Isobel in *A New Era*, "I was a fool for love in those days," before then explaining that she was happy with Robert's father, ". . . well, happy enough in that English way when you never talk about anything but you trust each other."

Her marriage to Patrick Crawley resulted in the birth of Robert, the current seventh Earl of Grantham, and daughter Rosamund, who would become Lady Rosamund Painswick. The family's increasing lack of funds meant that Robert had to find himself a wealthy wife, and he subsequently married American heiress Cora Levinson. Despite reaping the benefits of her daughter-in-law's fortune, Violet couldn't quite get used to what she described as a "peculiar marriage" and would delight in casting aspersions about Americans in general. As a result, she and Cora had many run-ins over the years. Gradually, the two have developed a respect for each other, born from their loyalty to the family. Violet even admits to Cora in her final scene of the film that she had been wrong about her, but it's only now that she can bring herself to say it.

Violet has seen a huge amount of change over her lifetime, which stretches from a Victorian childhood of crinolines and petticoats, horses, carriages, and candlelight to votes for women, rising hemlines, the first Labour government, and the advent of the motorcar, electric light, and the extraordinary array of technological innovations of the current period. Of Downton's newly installed telephone, Violet once remarked, "Is this an instrument of communication or torture?" And in her final days in the film, she muses on what she's seen in her life: "When I think about that world of long ago, when

"... life is a game, where the player must appear ridiculous."

–VIOLET GRANTHAM

I was a girl in my first crinoline . . . in those moments I feel as if I've been transported to a different planet."

Despite her horror when it comes to the breakdown of certain social conventions, reeling in the 1920s when Robert starts to pour himself a whiskey in the library before dinner, Violet learns to accept certain circumstances within her own family that she might once have thought impossible. She accepts and welcomes Edith's illegitimate daughter, Marigold, into the family, as she does former family chauffeur Tom Branson, with whom she eventually becomes friends. She once delighted in putting down the resolutely middle-class Isobel Merton, though Isobel proved more than capable of standing her ground, and the two positively reveled in their verbal spats. Despite this, the pair have grown fond of each other, and Violet chooses Isobel to go through her private letters, admitting, "I'd never known anyone whose opinion I could trust to be morally right, not for years, not since my mother died."

To the end, Violet is fiercely loyal to her family, referring to Robert as "my dearest boy," admitting that she was cleverer than he but he was kinder. She leaves Edith and Mary, her "wonderful granddaughters," both confident that their lives will be "happy and fruitful." As Julian Fellowes explains, "Violet is a positive person. She took her family through a difficult historical period, including the Great War, and they came out the other end. The Granthams will survive at Downton Abbey—and that's one of the most important elements she has passed on to her granddaughters. She has turned the Crawleys into a fighting family, and they've just got to get on with it."

In the final minutes of her life, Violet is her own inimitable self, with just enough breath in her to deliver the withering one-liners for which she is known. Violet asks Maud Bagshaw, with whom she has always had a patchy relationship, if she has come to check on whether she is on the way out; and to her maid, who is loudly weeping, she says, "Do stop that noise. I can't hear myself die." She has made everyone in the room not only weep but also smile, as Julian Fellowes describes: "It seemed to be important that we should know that Violet's sense of humor has not deserted her at the very end. There is something about her own death that is entertaining to her."

That final line marks the end of an unforgettable character whose presence and indomitable spirit will long be felt at Downton Abbey. And yet in the words of Julian Fellowes, "However individualist a character may be, however entertaining, however defined that character is, in the end what's important is that the family go on."

Violet is too unwell to attend Tom and Lucy's wedding and remains at Downton Abbey during the festivities.

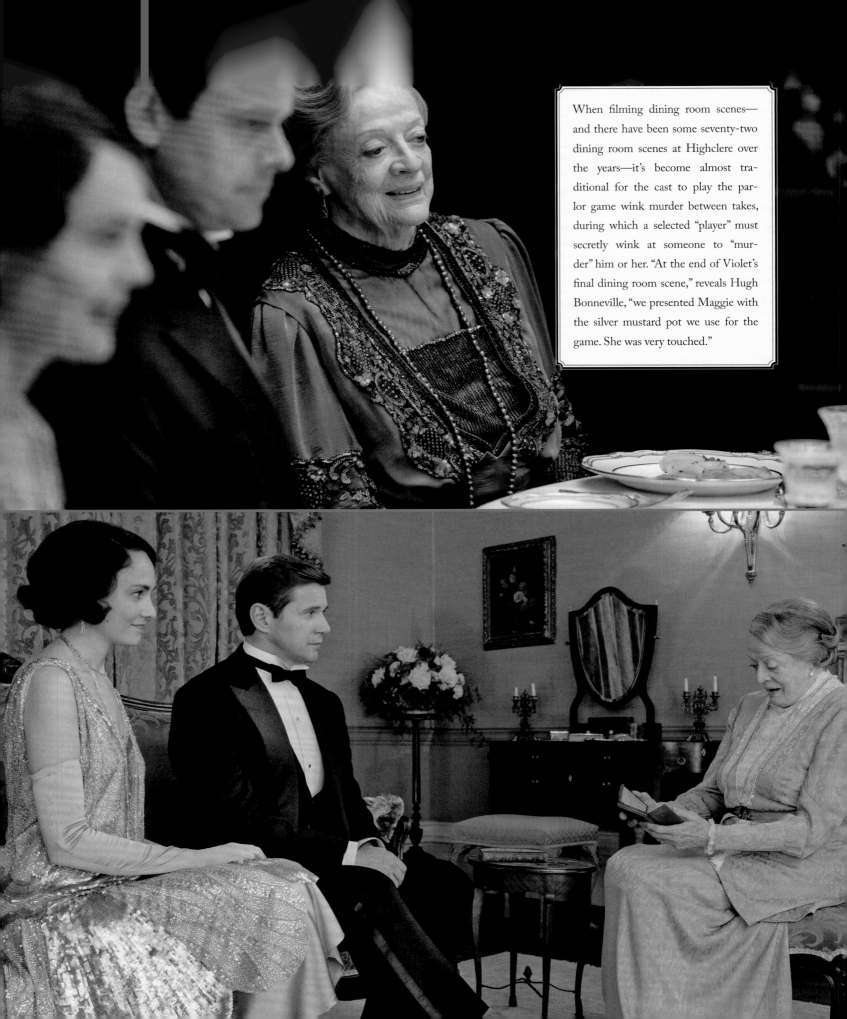

When filming dining room scenes—and there have been some seventy-two dining room scenes at Highclere over the years—it's become almost traditional for the cast to play the parlor game wink murder between takes, during which a selected "player" must secretly wink at someone to "murder" him or her. "At the end of Violet's final dining room scene," reveals Hugh Bonneville, "we presented Maggie with the silver mustard pot we use for the game. She was very touched."

**HARRY
HADDEN-PATON**
BERTIE

"The funeral was a real spectacle, with the whole village and household out on the drive. In filming, there was all this bluster and a few jokes, but when the camera was running, there was silence, and you start to reflect on what everyone had been through in making this show. The cast and crew are a big family, and there have been births and deaths and a lot has happened. It also gave us a chance to reflect on Dame Maggie and her remarkable career and what she brought to the world with this character."

DAME MAGGIE SMITH • *Actor*

THE ACTRESS WHO BRINGS THE CHARACTER of Violet, the Dowager Countess to life is Dame Maggie Smith, one of the United Kingdom's most distinguished actresses in theater, film, and television. Across six decades, her notable achievements have included Desdemona in *Othello* opposite Laurence Olivier in 1964; the title role in *The Prime of Miss Jean Brodie* in 1969, for which she won an Academy Award; the snobbish Countess of Trentham in *Gosford Park* (2001), in a screenplay for which Julian Fellowes would receive an Oscar and on whom the character of Violet was partly based; and witchcraft teacher Minerva McGonagall in the *Harry Potter* series of films.

As Violet in *Downton Abbey*, there is something of a strange alchemy that occurs when Maggie Smith delivers the lines that Julian Fellowes has created for her. "She understands why every line is there," says Julian, "and also of course she's very funny, so if you give her a line that has the potential to be funny, you never have to explain it." Funniest of these are the Dowager's stinging put-downs, which Maggie delivers to perfection. But she can then, in the next beat, convey real sadness or poignancy, which is a testament to her skills as an actress. Nicholas Hytner, who directed Maggie Smith in both the stage play and the 2015 film of *The Lady in the Van*, once said, "She can capture in a single moment more than many actors can convey in an entire film," and her final scene in *Downton Abbey:*

"She is so much at the heart of Downton. *"*

A New Era is a fine example of this.

When Dame Maggie is on the *Downton Abbey* set, there is always something of a charged atmosphere, felt even by veteran director Simon Curtis: "You always know when it's a Maggie Day. You're aware you're watching one of the greatest actors of all time at work. It's a tremendous privilege." She also has something of a mischievous sense of humor. She delighted in making Hugh Dancy (Jack Barber) laugh during filming and jokily berated David Robb (Dr. Clarkson) for his cold hands when lifting her hand to check her pulse.

Saying goodbye to such a defining character and actress proved emotional for everyone on set, including Dame Maggie herself. "When we shot Violet's final scene, I don't think there was a dry eye across the cast and crew that day," says producer Liz Trubridge. "She is so much at the heart of *Downton* that it felt very strange for all of us. In addition, Ros Rosenberg, who had worked as Maggie's stand-in throughout the series, insisted on making filming despite having just lost her husband, so it added more poignancy to the whole thing."

Director Simon Curtis also described filming Violet's death scene as "tremendously emotional. We were saying goodbye to Violet, and this was Maggie's final day of the shoot. The actors in playing a family have become something of a family themselves over the years, and we were all thinking of loved ones we may have lost in our own lives."

Nonetheless, never one to wallow in self-pity and not wanting to be like "one of those guests who packs the car but never leaves," Violet's end is very quick. Dame Maggie inhabits the character of Violet so completely that one feels she would also approve of the note of optimism at the end of *A New Era*. "The point is, I'll be fine until I'm not," she said to Mary in the previous movie. "That's all there is to it."

Isobel and Violet are a formidable pair, and while they frequently disagreed, they developed a close bond.

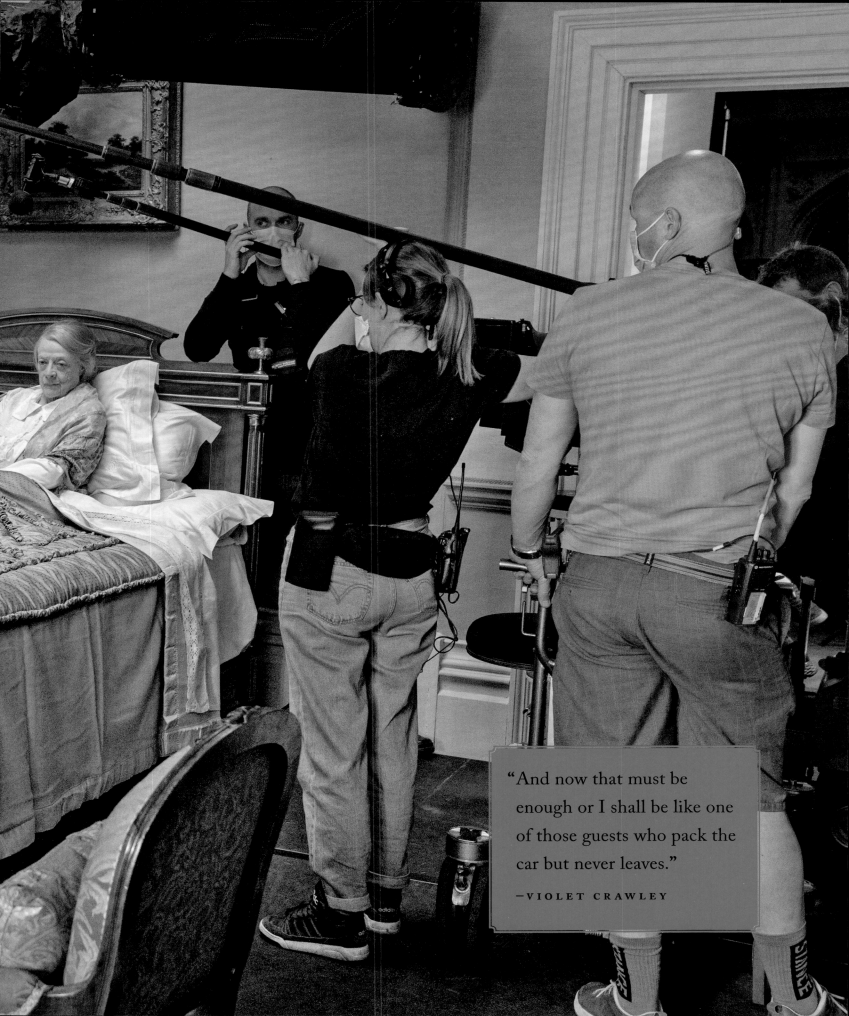

"And now that must be enough or I shall be like one of those guests who pack the car but never leaves."

—VIOLET CRAWLEY

LIZ TRUBRIDGE
PRODUCER

"When we shot Violet's final scene, I don't think there was a dry eye across the cast and crew that day. She selflessly made it all about her stand-in Ros, who has worked with her throughout the whole series."

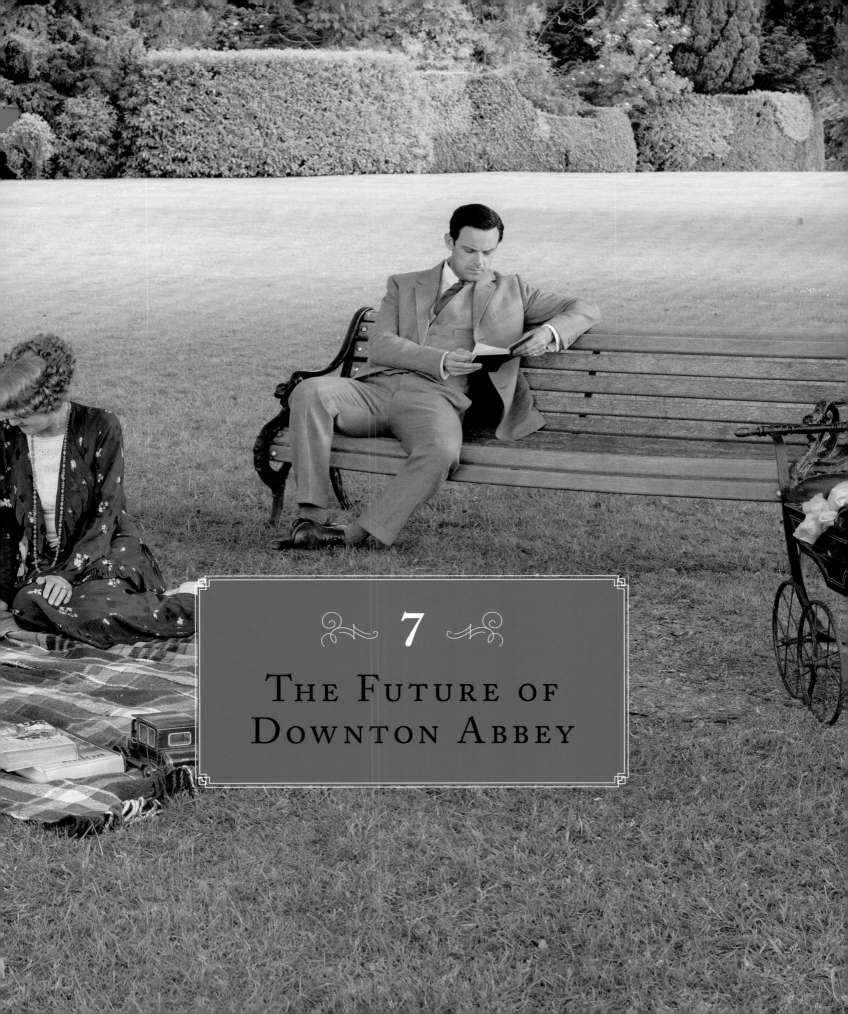

7

THE FUTURE OF
DOWNTON ABBEY

Children now happily run up and down the corridors and play on the grounds of Downton Abbey, and it is they, along with the most recent arrival, Tom and Lucy's new baby, who represent the future of the Crawley family.

Sybbie is the eldest grandchild of Lady Grantham and Lord Grantham, or Donk, as Sybbie calls Robert, a nickname given to him after a game of pin the tail on the donkey. Born in 1920, Sybbie is the daughter of Tom Branson and her namesake, Sybil, Robert and Cora's youngest daughter, who died in childbirth of eclampsia. After a brief period away, Sybbie grew up largely on the Downton estate and now lives with her father and his new wife, Lucy, at Brompton Park.

Fifi Hart, who has played the role of Sybbie since the beginning of season five, is a familiar figure on set. In *A New Era*, Violet makes the decision to bequeath the French villa of the late Marquis de Montmirail to her great-granddaughter Sybbie because she recognizes that, compared with her cousins, Sybbie will inherit little in the way of property, and Violet has a mind to correct that.

Heir presumptive to the Downton estate and the Earl of Grantham title is George Crawley, or Georgie as his mother, Lady Mary, calls him. He is the son of Mary's first husband, Matthew Crawley, who died on the day of his birth, and Henry Talbot is now his stepfather. Lord Grantham's father created an entail for Downton Abbey that decreed that the title and estate, including Cora's fortune, would be passed down to the nearest male heir, who is now George Crawley. Before he died, George's father, Matthew, bought half the estate, which is not part of the entail, and Mary now owns that part of the estate. On her death, her share will also pass to George.

Now at seven years old, George is played by identical twins Oliver and Zac Barker. It's not unusual for film productions to cast twins in the role of children, as working hours on set can be unpredictable and long, and alternating twins for the same role enables the production team to build in adequate rest, eating, tutoring, and playtime for the children.

The third grandchild of Robert and Cora is Marigold, played by Eva and Karina Samms. Now aged six, she is the daughter of Lady Edith and the late Michael Gregson. As Edith was unmarried when she had Marigold, there were attempts to hide her birth and identity, but Edith couldn't bear to be apart from her daughter, and Marigold was eventually brought to Downton Abbey and welcomed by the family. Some feared that knowledge of Marigold's illegitimacy

Sybbie will inherit little in the way of property, and Violet has a mind to correct that.

would prevent Bertie Pelham, a high-ranking marquess, from marrying Edith, but he was undeterred, and Marigold now lives with her mother and stepfather at Brancaster Castle with her new baby brother, Peter, who is just one year old.

The daughter of Henry and Lady Mary, Caroline Talbot, who was born in 1926, is the younger half sister of George and the first grandchild of Robert and Cora to have both parents living. In the movie, Caroline is the youngest bridesmaid at Tom and Lucy's wedding, with Marigold and Sybbie, and her brother, George, is a page boy.

Johnny Bates, son of Mr. Bates and Anna, was born at Downton Abbey on New Year's Eve 1925, the same day that Lady Edith and Bertie Pelham married. Johnny lives with his mother and father at their cottage (and is cared for in the Downton nursery). In *A New Era*, Mr.

Bates leaves Johnny with Anna when he heads off to the South of France.

As older generations pass, more children will arrive at Downton Abbey, and the nursery, hallways, and drawing rooms will fill with new voices. Downton is more than just a grand house; it is a home to the Crawley family and their servants, and life will continue within its walls. Lord Grantham and his parents before him were temporary custodians of the house and estate, and they always knew they had a duty to preserve it for the next generation.

At the end of the movie, we see Tom and Lucy arrive with their new baby—a baby that marks the most recent addition to the new generation and the story of Downton Abbey. As the family cluster around the baby, a portrait of the Dowager Countess looks on, a reminder that, as Cora put it to Robert, ". . . individual Crawleys come and go. But the family lives on. Mama knew that and believed in it."

ABOVE Tom's daughter, Sybbie, is to inherit the French Villa des Colombes from her great-grandmother Violet. **OPPOSITE** Sybbie and Lady Mary's son, George, often help out in the kitchen, where Mrs. Patmore and Daisy frequently spoil them with sweet treats.

Sybbie, George (wearing a black arm band), and Edith's daughter, Marigold, watch as the funeral procession for their great-grandmother leaves Downton Abbey.

Cora, her sister-in-law, Rosamund, and Edith share happy times with Sybbie and Marigold.

ABOVE Mr. Bates couldn't be happier, with his wife, Anna, and son, Johnny. OPPOSITE TOP Lady Mary holds Caroline, who was a bridesmaid at Tom and Lucy's wedding. OPPOSITE BOTTOM Tom and Lucy arrive with the most recent addition to Downton Abbey.

weldon**owen**

An imprint of Insight Editions

CEO Raoul Goff
VP Publisher Roger Shaw
Associate Publisher Amy Marr
Editorial Assistant Jourdan Plautz
VP Creative Chrissy Kwasnik
Art Director Allister Fein
Editorial Director Katie Killebrew
VP Manufacturing Alix Nicholaeff
Production Manager Sam Taylor
Sr. Production Mgr, Subsidiary Rights Lina s Palma-Tenema

Produced by Weldon Owen
P.O. Box 3088
San Rafael, CA 94912
www.weldonowen.com

ISBN: 978-1-68188-821-7

Printed in China
10 9 8 7 6 5 4 3 2 1

Weldon Owen wishes to thank Gareth Neame, Margaret Parvin, Charlotte Fay, Nion Hazell, and Wai-Lan Lam at Carnival Films; Megan Startz and Melissa Rodriguez at NBCUniversal; Amy Rivera at Focus Features; and Annabel Merullo and Daisy Chandley at Peters Fraser + Dunlop; Rachel Markowitz, Elizabeth Parson, and Sharon Silva.

FROM THE AUTHOR

Once again, it has been a real pleasure to talk to the remarkable team behind Downton Abbey. My thanks in particular to Gareth Neame, Julian Fellowes, Liz Trubridge, Simon Curtis, Laraine Porter, Anna Mary Scott Robbins, Anne "Nosh" Oldham, Donal Woods, Mark "Sparky" Ellis, Charlotte Fay and to all the cast members who spoke about life on a Downton Abbey film set. At Weldon Owen, my thanks to Roger Shaw, Amy Marr, and Allister Fein.

Picturegoer and *Film Weekly* courtesy of Rebellion. Used under license. All rights reserved.

The Terror Poster licensed by Warner Bros. Entertainment Inc.

Alamy: Ivy Close top left, bottom left, bottom right (15), Queen Victoria (88), George Murphy and Sara, Beatrice Lillie and Noël Coward (93), movie posters (112), Napoléon (114), Blackmail (116), Jean Harlow and Constance Bennett (124), Duncan Grant (137), Dorothy Gish, Clara Bow, Douglas Fairbanks, Charlie Chaplin, Ivor Novello, and Betty Balfour (176), Vilma Bánky (177)

Anna Mary Scott Robbins: wedding dress sketch (78), Edith's clothing sketch (124)

Donal Woods: concept sketches (95)

Gareth Neame: Ivy Close top right (15)

All third-party trademarks are the property of their respective owners.

ABOUT THE AUTHOR

Emma Marriott is the author of more than 15 high-profile popular histories and other non-fiction books, including the official companion to the first *Downton Abbey* movie, *The World of Vanity Fair*, and *The World of Poldark*. A former in-house editor at Pan Macmillan in London, Emma lives in Bedfordshire, England.